Cloud-Native Modernization Unleashed

Revolutionizing Legacy Systems with Spring, AI, Cloud, and Microservices

Mrinmoy Aich
Diganta Sengupta

Apress®

Cloud-Native Modernization Unleashed: Revolutionizing Legacy Systems with Spring, AI, Cloud, and Microservices

Mrinmoy Aich (ID)
Austin, TX, USA

Diganta Sengupta
Austin, TX, USA

ISBN-13 (pbk): 979-8-8688-2378-7
https://doi.org/10.1007/979-8-8688-2379-4

ISBN-13 (electronic): 979-8-8688-2379-4

Managing Director, Apress Media LLC: Welmoed Spahr
Acquisitions Editor: Celestin Suresh John
Editorial Assistant: Gryffin Winkler

Cover designed by eStudioCalamar

Distributed to the book trade worldwide by Springer Science+Business Media New York, 1 New York Plaza, New York, NY 10004. Phone 1-800-SPRINGER, fax (201) 348-4505, e-mail orders-ny@ springer-sbm.com, or visit www.springeronline.com. Apress Media, LLC is a Delaware LLC and the sole member (owner) is Springer Science + Business Media Finance Inc (SSBM Finance Inc). SSBM Finance Inc is a **Delaware** corporation.

For information on translations, please e-mail booktranslations@springernature.com; for reprint, paperback, or audio rights, please e-mail bookpermissions@springernature.com.

Apress titles may be purchased in bulk for academic, corporate, or promotional use. eBook versions and licenses are also available for most titles. For more information, reference our Print and eBook Bulk Sales web page at http://www.apress.com/bulk-sales.

Any source code or other supplementary material referenced by the author in this book is available to readers on GitHub. For more detailed information, please visit https://www.apress. com/gp/services/source-code.

If disposing of this product, please recycle the paper

*This book is dedicated to my wife, **Rimi Aich**, and my daughters, **Mrigakshi Aich** and **Rajika Aich**, whose constant support and encouragement made this work possible. Their patience, understanding, and unwavering belief in my efforts provided the foundation needed to reflect on and articulate the professional experiences presented in this book. My wife's steadfast motivation and my daughters' inspiring curiosity continually influenced my commitment to learning, innovation, and knowledge sharing. This book stands as a testament not only to a journey in cloud-native modernization but also to the enduring support of the family who made that journey meaningful.*

—Mrinmoy Aich

To my wife, Samyukta Sengupta, and my two little kids—Ishaan and Adrita—for their love, patience, and constant support, and to all those who inspired, guided, and believed in me along this journey—this book is for you!

—Diganta Sengupta

Table of Contents

Chapter 8: Monitoring Microservices with Prometheus and Grafana

Chapter 9: AI and Machine Learning in Modern Applications 177

About the Authors

 **Mrinmoy Aich** is an accomplished visionary technology leader with more than 25 years of experience in **software architecture, cloud computing, artificial intelligence, and supply chain logistics**. Renowned for his ability to **modernize legacy enterprise systems**, he has pioneered the adoption of **cloud-native architectures, microservices, and AI-driven automation** that enable organizations to scale efficiently, improve resilience, and drive **sustainable digital innovation**.

His expertise extends across **multi-cloud strategy, enterprise integration, and cloud security**, with a proven record of delivering **mission-critical platforms** for global enterprises.

A **Fellow and Fellowship Assessor of BCS, The Chartered Institute for IT**, and an **IEEE Senior Member**, he is also recognized as a mentor, thought leader, and author. His professional journey reflects not only **technical excellence** but also dedication to **knowledge sharing and talent development**, empowering teams and organizations to thrive in an era of rapid technological change.

Diganta Sengupta is a thought leader and technology strategist and a Forbes Technology Council member leader, specializing in AI, cloud, and blockchain-driven digital transformation. With over 25 years of experience, he has led large-scale innovations across manufacturing, energy, and utilities—modernizing systems for Fortune 500 organizations. He is a published researcher, thought leader, and passionate advocate for building trusted, intelligent enterprise ecosystems.

As a Master Principal Architect at Oracle, he has successfully led multi-million-dollar initiatives across highly regulated sectors—including oil and gas, utilities, manufacturing, and public infrastructure—delivering scalable, secure, and business-aligned solutions.

A trusted advisor to CIOs and CTOs, Diganta blends technical depth with strategic insight, shaping go-to-market strategies and governance models. He is a published researcher, IEEE Senior and ACM, BCS Fellow, and Forbes Technology Council leader—passionate about leveraging emerging tech to build connected, resilient, and intelligent enterprises.

About the Technical Reviewer

Mohammed Ilyas Ahmed is a senior security executive renowned for his leadership in DevSecOps and cloud-native architecture, helping organizations fortify their security postures at scale. With deep domain expertise and a track record of strategic impact, he guides enterprise teams through complex transformations in cybersecurity, compliance, and cloud environments.

He is a globally sought-after keynote presenter—appearing at events such as DEF CON, KubeCon Paris, and IANS—and regularly serves as a judge for technical sessions, reinforcing his role as an industry influencer. His research contributions at Harvard University, coupled with his membership on the Harvard Business Review Advisory Council, reflect his commitment to bridging academia and enterprise practice in security and innovation.

On the international stage, Mohammed serves as a member of the Global Advisory Board at VigiTrust Limited in Dublin, Ireland, shaping global cybersecurity and data protection strategies. His extensive professional certifications and credentials underscore his commitment to excellence and thought leadership in the field.

Beyond his enterprise work, he authored *Cloud-Native DevOps*, a practical guide to building scalable, secure cloud-native applications, further demonstrating his influence on technology strategy and developer practices.

Mohammed's core interests include cybersecurity, cloud-native technologies, DevSecOps, risk management, and the integration of artificial intelligence in cloud-native ecosystems.

CHAPTER 1

Introduction to Application Modernization

Application modernization is the process of updating and improving older software systems. It brings new life to systems built with outdated tools. Modernization helps meet current business needs and use today's technologies. In this chapter, we explain why modernization is needed, what it means, its benefits, and the challenges it brings. We also discuss how to choose the right technology and build a clear modernization roadmap.

Modern application formats are the tools through which organizations empower themselves to optimize and advance their ski programs, bringing them in line with contemporary operational and technological standards. The delay in modernization was due to the limitations of old technology, which suffered from inefficient operation, expensive maintenance requirements, and increasing security risks. However, modernization breathes new life into these systems, implementing cutting-edge technologies like cloud computing, microservices, and containerization and giving organizations a sense of control over their technological destiny.

M. Aich and D. Sengupta, *Cloud-Native Modernization Unleashed,*
https://doi.org/10.1007/979-8-8688-2379-4_1

Industry-modernized applications are not just a choice but a necessity for businesses to acquire better performance quality, scalability, and more substantial security features alongside cost efficiencies. The modernization process is not just about survival but about thriving in the face of market competition throughout changes in the digital landscape. Failure to modernize will force companies to keep using dated infrastructure, putting their survival at risk by diminishing their innovative abilities and response speed for market needs.

This chapter delves into the strategic necessity of modernizing applications, its fundamental principles, and the strategic business benefits resulting from this approach. Throughout this text, we explore the typical issues that affect businesses during modernization initiatives and present strategic strategies to address them. Our guidance includes the necessary steps for choosing appropriate modernization methods, including rehosting, replatforming, and rearchitecting, ensuring smooth process transitions. A detailed modernization roadmap serves as the final step that helps organizations strategically navigate through legacy system upgrade complexities to reduce risks and disturbances.

The Need for Modernization

What Is Application Modernization?

Old software systems transform application modernization to meet present-day technological criteria. The procedure uses legacy application modification to achieve improved functionality alongside better security and ease of maintenance, which delivers solutions that match contemporary business requirements. Organizations continue running software developed during past decades and throughout previous years. These outdated systems operate correctly but encounter difficulties when working with contemporary technologies. Additionally, they struggle to adapt to current business expectations and grow properly. A lack of modernization leads companies to face efficiency losses, keeps maintenance expenses high, and exposes them to security threats.

Code modernization requires designers to research new designs alongside architectural changes for an application. Standard monolithic applications demonstrate both program fixedness and resistance to easy system updates. Modernization enables converting these applications into modular microservices by creating independent component structures. The partial system organization enables developers to perform application fixes or updates in individual sections rather than impacting the entire program, which results in speedier deployments, increased flexibility, and decreased downtime.

Modernization includes the fundamental practice of cloud migration as one of its key components. Hard-to-operate physical servers are expensive for legacy systems because they were developed before cloud technology emerged. Businesses benefit from cloud-based environments when they move applications because they receive scalable infrastructure with automated updates and cost reductions. Cloud-native applications have a better capacity to handle increased user traffic, delivering steady performance and reliability features.

The modernization process strengthens the ability of systems to collaborate with state-of-the-art technological solutions. The current applications can integrate artificial intelligence and machine learning with data analytics easily, enabling businesses to achieve better insights while processing automation and making enhanced decisions. Current systems that have been revamped provide better features for data management alongside processing functions while becoming safer and more efficient.

Modernized applications are essential because software needs updates to thrive in today's rapidly changing digital market. Through business modernization practices, technology remains adaptable and cost-effective while preparing for future advancements. Onboarded modernization enables organizations to provide more efficient user experiences, streamline operations, and decrease security problems from legacy systems.

Why Do Legacy Applications Become Obsolete?

The programming languages, architectural designs, and principles used in legacy applications no longer match the modern requirements of business structures. Items built for unique environments, hardware, and operational models of the past remain obsolete even though technologies have progressed. Businesses obtained practical functionality from legacy applications prior; however, their failure to transform into modern technology creates serious operational problems.

Legacy applications become outmoded because of their inflexibility. The design approach of older systems includes tight coupling among components, which results in extensive interconnection between system elements. System updates, modifications, and scalability become problematic because single modifications in one part frequently cause unintended issues that spread across the entire system. Businesses require higher flexibility and adaptability while expanding, so monolithic legacy applications become undesirable assets.

Cloud-based infrastructures encounter severe support difficulties, a fundamental problem among many legacy systems today. Businesses face significant challenges when using legacy applications that run on physical servers on-premises because such infrastructure entails high operational and expansion costs. The increasing trend toward cloud computing has caused businesses to require applications that address cloud-based storage, power, and security capabilities. Older applications usually do not provide enough architectural elements to join cloud services, making companies decide between running expensive on-site systems or performing time-consuming redesigns.

The high maintenance costs of legacy systems are significant factors in their replacement with newer technologies. Because technology progresses rapidly, becoming skilled at recently obsolete programming codes and software systems remains expensive. The maintenance of specialists who handle older technologies creates additional expenses for companies. Organizations deal with escalating financial expenses because they must maintain obsolete hardware that supports these applications.

The integration problems between new and outdated systems quicken the aging process of legacy applications. Current businesses need connected frameworks with APIs and instant data-sharing platforms because these elements enable operation efficiency and strengthen customer interactions. Businesses encounter integration challenges when using legacy applications with newer systems because these applications lack required communication interfaces, thus making emerging technologies challenging to adopt, including artificial intelligence (AI), big data analytics, and automation. Businesses using modern integrated solutions advance beyond those that must maintain legacy application systems because these systems prevent efficiency and innovation.

Businesses must also address the growing number of security weaknesses in their infrastructure. Applications from past years fail to upgrade their security precautions, which results in vulnerability to cyberattacks. Attackers specifically choose old digital systems because these systems maintain recognized security weaknesses, which hackers convert into breaches, financial thefts, and system failures. Using antique software for business operations makes compliance with current security regulations burdensome, thus exposing organizations to potential legal consequences and monetary fines.

Legacy applications lose their practical value because of their rigid design, inability to work with contemporary computing systems, high support expenses, integration complexities, and multiple security risks. Snapping up businesses in today's digital landscape requires application modernization since it provides essential benefits for performance enhancement, improved security, and enhanced scalability. Organizations that choose newer technologies and cloud-based solutions create a future-proof IT infrastructure that helps them better adjust to evolving market requirements.

Tightly Coupled Codebases

The different code components found in legacy systems are highly dependent. A minimal transformation to a section in the system triggers modifications throughout its various parts. Adding new features together with updates results in complicated development tasks. The entire system faces potential risks during changes in its design. These risks, if not addressed, can lead to significant setbacks. However, they also present an opportunity for change and the potential benefits of modernization.

The primary challenge posed by tight coupling in codebases is the inability to separate modules. This results in a monolithic design approach, which is a fundamental architectural difference between legacy and contemporary applications based on microservices and loosely linked designs. The inherent connection between all system components necessitates a comprehensive examination of every part of the system when making even minimal alterations. This leads to extended development periods and increases the likelihood of new system failures or bugs during update implementations.

Synchronization issues emerge when systems have tight dependencies. Application development requires developers to understand every interconnected logic between system components to modify parts of the application successfully. Organizational onboarding for new developers becomes more arduous, while maintenance prices escalate after implementation. Businesses face difficulty with technological implementation and third-party service incorporation because the systems lack flexibility.

Updating an outdated ERP system, for instance, which links customer information, order processing, and inventory control functions through one central architecture, can be a complex task. Implementing advanced analytics tracking for customer behavior would require modifying many components throughout the system, potentially leading to unexpected system errors and delays. This highlights the need for modernization and the potential benefits it can bring.

Modern business operations, despite experiencing a slowdown due to the delay in swiftly matching software features to new operational needs, can find hope in modernization projects. These projects, which typically involve dividing monolithic apps into microservices alongside implementing container-based systems, offer a path to enhanced efficiency and reduced risks. They enable independent functionality of different application parts, which enhances update processes and reduces the risks involved with tightly interconnected code bases.

There is a direct relationship between rigid networked systems, which reduce scalability, increase costs, and delay innovation. This makes modernization work on existing applications vital for organizations wishing to stay competitive through market-responsive operations. It underscores the need for modernization and the potential benefits it can bring.

Lack of Cloud Compatibility

Most older business systems operated using physical on-premise servers. These systems do not operate effectively in cloud hosting platforms. Current cloud platform solutions provide users with adaptable and expandable platforms. Legacy systems find it difficult to exploit cloud advantages because they lack capabilities for cloud integration.

Cloud computing has fundamentally changed business operations, providing cost-effectiveness, scalability features, and easy access. Legacy applications maintain their original purpose, which becomes incompatible when developers utilize outdated technologies and architectural concepts to create these systems. The applications work with inflexible structures, thus presenting migration to cloud systems as a costly and complicated process.

The greatest barrier to cloud incompatibility arises from different architectural approaches. Modern applications that qualify as cloud-native utilize microservices technology together with containerization and API communications as their essential development structures. The architecture of legacy applications consists of a monolithic design that binds each component into a unified structure. A challenge arises from cloud deployment when developers cannot split functions independently from existing code because detailed restructuring is necessary.

Another issue is scalability. A cloud platform enables businesses to adjust their resource capacity by demand levels to receive optimal performance and budgetary advantages. Legacy applications were built for environments that use fixed hardware resources within stable environments. During periods of high usage, the non-elastically designed system creates performance problems that slow down operations and degrade user experience.

Security is a key issue that develops when transitioning legacy systems into the cloud environment. Cloud security standards require newer application features that older systems do not contain for authentication and encryption compliance standards. Organizations need to perform proper modifications when they move applications to prevent cyber threats and data breaches against their systems.

The outdated banking system implemented by a financial institution creates difficulties when trying to implement contemporary cloud-based security elements such as multi-factor authentication and AI-powered fraud detection technology. Unprepared organizations lack cloud compatibility, enabling their competitors to perform real-time analysis and benefit from automated security corrections.

The solution to these issues requires businesses to use modernization methods such as rehosting (applying a cloud migration), refactoring (revamping code), and rearchitecting (creating microservices-friendly systems). By addressing compatibility problems, organizations can maximize cloud computing benefits, enabling them to achieve enhanced operational speed and economic advantages. More importantly, these modernization methods open the door to creative developments in our present-day digital world, inspiring business leaders and IT professionals with the possibilities of innovation.

High Maintenance Costs

The support of old software programs carries massive maintenance costs. For instance, a company may need to pay significantly higher salaries to retain or attract professionals with expertise in outdated technologies. The support system requires highly specialized expertise and hardware components operating on older designs. Current technology developments elevate the expenses needed for sustaining and updating such systems, and these systems demonstrate lower cost-effectiveness with each passing year.

Maintaining legacy systems proves to be a significant challenge due to the scarcity of professionals with expertise in antiquated programming languages and obsolete frameworks. Organizations are faced with the daunting task of maintaining older applications that utilize outdated technologies such as COBOL, FORTRAN, or VB6. The growing challenges in locating professionals who possess the expertise needed to support aging systems are a clear indication of the urgency of the situation. Labor costs rise steeply because experienced professionals who maintain older technologies command high prices in the job market.

Personnel costs increase due to the need for technical maintenance of legacy systems, which also demands investing in outdated hardware replacement or repair. The initial design of numerous older applications made them functional on physical servers instead of cloud-based or virtual environments. The end of manufacturer support for outmoded equipment forces companies to spend substantial funds to maintain outdated systems. System downtime from hardware breakdowns not only interrupts operations but also results in significant monetary losses for business operations, emphasizing the potential financial implications.

Businesses spend more on maintenance operations because their legacy systems are complex technological structures. The architectural structure of present-day systems relies on modules, whereas former applications used tied-up integration throughout their elements. System components cannot be updated independently because all parts are tightly connected, resulting in modifications spreading through the whole system. The testing process for minor alterations and debugging routines extends development time while raising project expenses.

Security-related challenges raise expenses connected to maintenance. The older a system becomes, the higher its risk for cyberattacks grows because vendors stop providing security updates and updates. Organizations need to buy tailored security systems that secure critical information while fulfilling regulatory standards in their industry. The lack of proper security measures will lead to data breaches while bringing legal sanctions and damaging customer trust.

Medical facilities facing challenges with modern security implementation experience difficulties due to using an outdated patient management system. The organization must either pay specialists or create expensive solutions to protect the system, resulting in higher expenses.

Businesses should urgently consider implementing modernization approaches that include system replatforming to more budget-friendly infrastructure, reengineering critical elements with contemporary technology, or completely replacing their present system. Modernization is not just an option, but a necessity that enables businesses to decrease operational costs, increase efficiency, and liberate resources for innovation efforts that surpass maintenance expenses.

Limited Integration Capabilities

Today, businesses operate with APIs and microservices to establish system linkages and distribute data between them. Modern business applications usually do not possess these capabilities. The systems were not constructed to allow painless communication with current systems. The business faces restricted innovation potential along with limited integration of new services.

The main difficulty with legacy applications emerges from their controlled design structure. The original designs of numerous aging systems created them as independent entities that did not enable connections to external platforms and third-party applications. The core functionality of legacy applications depends on antiquated communication protocols that regulate database links through proprietary methods instead of using RESTful APIs and event-driven or web services. The consequent difficulty prevents legacy systems from linking with current business tools such as customer relationship management (CRM) systems, enterprise resource planning (ERP) software, and cloud-based analytics platforms.

The absence of integration capabilities proves an obstacle to companies that want to boost their digital transformation process. Existing businesses need real-time data exchange and automation to optimally use resources to expand customer satisfaction and gain market advantages. Systems of the past that lacked complete integration functionality form distinct data territories that keep vital departmental information separated from the rest of the organization. An outdated inventory system in retail operations prevents companies from establishing connections between their e-commerce platform—an integration deficit results in inventory misalignment, slow customer order management, and poor customer service quality.

The main shortcoming arises from the lack of capability to harness new technological advancements. Modern business solutions implement AI, ML features, and IoT technologies. These ancient systems fail to implement the essential interfaces with sufficient computing power, prohibiting them from adopting modern technologies. Organizations running legacy systems eliminate important opportunities to streamline business procedures, optimize decision systems, and improve customer connections.

Security is a pressing issue when it comes to legacy systems that lack integration features. The current standard for software authentication security, which uses OAuth and token-based authentication, is not met by these systems. Instead, they rely on insecure file transfers, hardcoded credentials, and outdated encryption methods, leading to serious security risks and potential compliance violations.

These issues can be solved through three modernization approaches: API enablement, middleware integration, and complete system migration. It's important to remember that organizations achieving innovation and efficiency obtain flexible system ecosystems through cloud-based services and microservices architectures. Therefore, it's crucial for organizations to consider these modernization strategies, as those that refuse to modernize risk losing ground to competitors who have already adopted digital transformation and developed systems that function without hindrance.

Security Risks

The risk of cyberattacks gravitates more toward systems that remain un-upgraded. Such applications never receive official updates or security patches, so they remain exposed to attacks due to their outdated state. Security gaps between systems allow attackers to perform breaches and create operational risks.

The most significant security problem with legacy applications stems from their absence of routine updates. Regular updates are crucial as they prevent new threats from entering systems. Modern software vendors create and send out these updates that solve vulnerabilities, making them a necessary practice. The official support that legacy systems receive ends, making them defenseless against modern cyberattacks. At present, hackers take advantage of program weaknesses by launching ransomware, malware, and phishing attacks against out-of-date software.

Security becomes a problem when organizations continue to operate with previous security standards. Operating systems from the past did not employ today's encryption standards or authentication protocols. Security vulnerabilities persist in older systems because they continue employing insecure methods for password management, unencrypted data transfers, and embedded credentials, creating opportunities for hackers to exploit them. MFA and RBAC security protocols are essential because their absence enables unauthorized users to access business-sensitive data, leading to financial losses as well as damage to organizational reputation.

Businesses face compliance challenges because of their legacy computer applications. Companies in finance and healthcare must follow data protection rules such as GDPR, HIPAA, and PCI-DSS because their industries have strict regulations. The absence of modern security capabilities within legacy systems causes companies to violate legal requirements, resulting in legal consequences and possible court actions. The operation of such a hospital becomes at risk due to a data breach stemming from a patient records system with insufficient encryption, which results in financial penalties and decreased trust from patients.

The monolithic structure of older systems creates substantial difficulties when trying to monitor and secure them. Present-day security frameworks contrast older systems, which display poor visibility toward security events. Such systems reduce the speed at which threats can be identified before they escalate into damages. The lack of proper logging and alert systems prevents organizations from recognizing their system compromises until it becomes too late for a response.

Modern applications are necessary for business organizations to reduce these security threats. A business should use middleware solutions and secure cloud environments or choose to replace its outdated technologies with modern, secure alternatives to perform security patch implementations. Companies should support data security by investing in encryption solutions, AI detection technologies, and zero-trust security frameworks because these not only protect businesses from contemporary cyber threats but also enhance operational efficiency, improve customer trust, and ensure regulatory compliance.

Legacy application security vulnerabilities should receive immediate attention. Neglecting them leads to costly financial damages and possible legal consequences. However, by implementing modernized IT infrastructure, businesses can gain enhanced security protection, compliance, and effective defense against rising cyber threats to their valuable data, reassuring them about potential positive outcomes.

Example: Legacy ERP System and Modernization Challenges

A retail business adopts one type of monolithic enterprise resource planning system that covers all of its operations. The old system was created 20 years ago to supervise essential business areas such as inventory tracking, financial management, and supply chain coordination. The software emerged as an advanced technological frontier at its creation time, giving the company unified capabilities to optimize its operational procedures.

As technology advanced and business needs changed, the company identified its ERP system as a growing point of limitation. The modern retail business uses AI-based demand forecasting because it helps businesses understand trends in customer behavior while maximizing their inventory. Cloud-based analytics allow real-time understanding of internal data, so decision leaders gain better control over operational success. The current business information system cannot integrate modern features because it fails to support APIs.

The company faces limited options because its lack of API compatibility requires manual data entries using outdated tools, which decreases operational speed and exposes the system to potential errors. For instance, during peak sales periods, the manual data entry process often leads to delays and inaccuracies, affecting customer satisfaction. The business also faces challenges handling seasonal demand shifts because it cannot utilize cloud infrastructure due to its inability to connect with cloud services. This has led to missed opportunities and increased costs during peak demand periods.

Security protocols in the ERP system remain vulnerable because they are outdated, even when faced with increasing cybersecurity threats. Due to the absence of regular patches or encryption updates, the business remains exposed to security breaches and unauthorized access to sensitive data such as customer transactions and supplier contracts.

The business is actively seeking different modernization solutions to address these recognized shortcomings. Implementing an API layer should be part of establishing connections with external applications. The company can move toward a microservice-based model through stages so each system component retains independence for updates or changes without impacting the complete system.

Through ERP system modernization, the company will gain new functional capabilities, achieve better security, and enhance the scalability of its systems. The modernized platform positions the company for success against changing retail market requirements and showcases its adaptability to new technologies, allowing it to utilize these for increased business expansion.

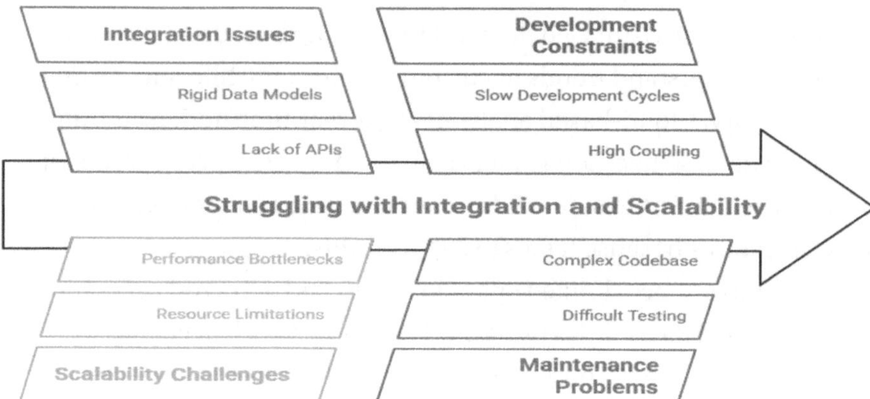

Figure 1-1. *A Simple Diagram Showing a Large, Tightly Coupled Monolithic Application Struggling with Integration and Scalability*

Benefits of Application Modernization

Modernizing an application is not only about adopting new technology. It is about future-proofing the business. The benefits are clear. Below are the key advantages of modernization:

Scalability and Performance

Modern times trigger proportional increases in business applications due to company growth. Systems with such structures handle both rising user numbers and expanding data collection. Each microservice enables the independent expansion of system components since it transforms large monolithic systems into standalone units. The system extends its size solely through areas that need to accommodate increased demand.

Systems that adapt to evolving user needs are crucial for businesses in today's digital landscape, as these needs translate into vital market demands. Unlike monolithic systems, microservices alleviate the burden of system complexity when scaling. With a monolithic system, all parts are intricately connected, so when one module needs to expand, the entire application must be upgraded, leading to increased costs and system complexity. The flexibility of microservices design mitigates these issues, preventing performance problems, delays, and system downtime during peak traffic.

The microservice architecture enables business-focused individual development of application components according to current needs. High levels of e-commerce website traffic begin when holiday sales start. Business expansion that requires changes to the entire platform framework would necessitate a complete reconfiguration when working with monolith-based systems. Thanks to microservices architecture, the checkout system and payment processing segment have scaling abilities to optimize transaction processing with maximum system efficiency.

Cloud computing empowers organizations to enhance scalability through overall performance improvements in their computing process. Cloud-structured applications automatically adjust resources based on observed traffic patterns, providing a level of adaptability that instills confidence. Companies can achieve superior results while reducing infrastructure costs by selectively using resources that match their operational needs.

When faced with CRM system performance issues during peak times, organizations can rely on cloud-based hosting solutions for a reliable performance boost. As usage levels fluctuate, the cloud platform automatically adjusts computational resources, ensuring faster response times throughout operations. This reliability translates to better customer service and a system configuration that workers can use easily.

Modern applications achieve their highest efficiency through the implementation of Docker and Kubernetes as containerization tools. Containerization is a lightweight form of virtualization that allows applications to be packaged with their dependencies and run in any environment. Applications inside containers allow more effortless transfer between environments because container dependency sets function as complete packages. When businesses want fast operation expansion, they achieve it by preventing compatibility issues during their growth period.

Combined application modernization strategies for scalability and performance enable organizations to deliver superior user operations and expand their business capacity effectively to maintain their market position. Businesses maintain future application protection by moving to cloud-native solutions, such as serverless computing or managed databases, reducing operational costs, and improving efficiency.

Cost Reduction and Resource Efficiency

The expansion of companies leads to a proportional growth of their business applications within the modern timescale. Systems incorporating this structure manage escalating active user counts and expanding data accumulations. Independent expansion of system components becomes possible through each microservice subdividing large monolithic systems into separate whole units. The system grows in size exclusively to meet demand requirements in particular portions.

Companies operating in digital markets require changeable systems to manage user requirements because evolving user requirements become vital market requirements at present. A monolithic system fails to perform well under scaling requirements since every system section needs direct connectivity to others. A system-wide update becomes necessary whenever a single application module wants to increase in size, leading to additional system cost and complexity. System performance issues with delays and system downtime incidents appear during peak traffic levels because of the inflexible system design.

The microservice architecture empowers developers, allowing them to create business-oriented application segments that meet current needs specifically and independently. As the holiday sales commence, e-commerce website traffic will reach its highest point. Any business expansion project that impacts the entire platform framework demands a complete platform reconfiguration due to monolith-based systems. The accompanying microservices architecture provides the checkout and payment processing segments with individual scaling systems to maximize system performance during transaction processing.

Cloud computing systems provide adaptable scalability and better performance across all computing systems, offering a sense of relief to organizations. Applications in a cloud structure scale up or down based on the traffic behaviors they detect. Organizations that opt to use just the necessary application resources receive exceptional performance while paying less for physical infrastructure.

Cloud-based solutions are the preferred choice for the organization to solve CRM system performance problems when volumes are high. Without human intervention, the cloud platform functions through natural resource modification processes to match changing usage patterns. The system operates with quicker response times during all stages of its procedures. The system becomes more reliable. Customers experience better service. The system takes on a shape that enables effortless worker use.

Applications reach maximum efficiency by implementing Docker with Kubernetes because they are containerized tools. Containerized applications help environment transfers because their complete dependency packages operate within containers. A quick operation growth model enables businesses to eliminate compatibility problems during expansion through proper planning, enhancing their productivity and effectiveness.

Organizations that use combined approaches for application modernization achieve superior user operations and effective business expansion to preserve their market position. Cloud-native solutions offer future protection to applications and introduce operational efficiencies and cost savings to businesses.

Faster Development and Deployment

Today's development practices expedite the entire software development period. CI/CD pipelines enhance updating software by enabling fast implementation. Update cycles now happen much faster than monolithic systems used to handle because major events no longer occur with each change.

The traditional software development method adopted a fixed waterfall system, requiring extended development processes, which required testing alongside manual deployment procedures. This process often caused delays and inefficiencies. Modernized applications have adopted DevOps principles to let developers conduct automatic testing followed by integration and deployment tasks. CI/CD pipelines help speed up system updates by permitting quick and dependable application of new features and bug fixes alongside security fixes.

Within a modernized approach, developers can create individual small parts of the system. Development in a single section remains independent from checking the total system operation. Organizations can apply system updates through shorter maintenance windows following this approach. Modern software systems require extensive periods to update the basic features of supply chain management tools. The modernized system enables individual updates of each feature. The speed of development results in additional system updates throughout a shorter period. The business gains the capability to adapt fast to market alterations.

Combining Docker and Kubernetes tools under the concept of containerization helps expedite the entire development process from start to finish. Application deployment through these tools produces uniform movement across different environments, eliminating deployment hazards and decreasing compatibility concerns. A business that uses Infrastructure as Code automation obtains automated infrastructure deployment while maintaining consistent environments across different deployment locations.

Businesses obtain manufacturing speedups that help them develop novel solutions, boost program reliability, and stay ahead in dynamic marketplaces.

Seamless Integration with AI, APIs, and Cloud Services

Today's applications are developed with built-in integration capabilities. Such applications create user-friendly connections to third-party platforms. Applications gain access to AI services through this significant benefit. Computers use artificial intelligence to execute recurring operations and extract data-based strategic information from digital sources.

Artificial intelligence is an essential factor in current business management practices. Business-enabled applications use AI models to measure customer actions, forecast marketplace evolutions, and execute repetitious tasks. AI-driven chatbots provide advanced support for customers through their deployment, while machine learning algorithms operate effectively to detect financial system fraud. Modern applications cannot harness AI developments because of non-modernized legacy systems.

APIs (application programming interfaces) create a system that enables diverse software programs to exchange information. Currently deployed applications exchange data with their connected services through API gateways, integrating the business environment more. Implementing RESTful APIs, GraphQL, and WebSockets enables modern software solutions to provide smooth intercommunication between different operational systems.

A modernized application enables an e-commerce business to add AI recommendation engines that pair with real-time payment systems and third-party logistics capabilities through API connections. The application delivers improved operational effectiveness through better service execution, helping customers achieve optimal experiences.

Cloud services enable organizations to use remote storage together with adjustable computing capabilities. The system allows users access to sophisticated analytic platforms and automated functions. Clients who choose the cloud can activate computing resources with extensive data storage capabilities and AI-based analytics tools when required—the absence of physical infrastructure cuts down expenses while granting organizations improved flexibility when managing data-heavy processing operations.

Through these integration methods, businesses gain the ability to build novel, innovative services that they can offer to their customers. These improved financial apps can link with security detection solutions in the cloud, which offer client-specific financial analysis and instant security reactions.

Adopting present-day integration capabilities enables organizations to sustain technical progress while enhancing operational efficiency for developing flexible software products that respond to customer market changes.

Enhanced Security and Compliance

Security is a foremost priority in today's digital landscape. Modern applications are built with up-to-date security measures. They often include:

- **OAuth and JWT Authentication:** These methods secure access to the application.

- **Role-Based Access Control (RBAC):** This restricts access to sensitive areas based on user roles.

- **Encryption for Data at Rest and in Transit:** Data is protected whether it is stored or being sent.

- **Regular Security Patches:** Automated CI/CD pipelines help keep the system secure with frequent updates.

By following modern security best practices, organizations can reduce the risk of cyber threats. They also ensure compliance with rules such as GDPR and HIPAA. This builds trust with customers and partners.

Challenges in Modernization

Modernization is important, but it does not come without challenges. Organizations need to be prepared for difficulties as they update their systems. Here are the main challenges:

Resistance to Change

Change is often met with resistance. Developers and IT teams may be used to the old way of doing things. They might fear that new architectures or cloud technologies will be too complex. Employees may worry about the need for retraining. This resistance can slow down the modernization strategy.

- **Example:** An IT team might prefer the known challenges of the old system rather than face the uncertainty of a new approach.

- **Solution:** Clear communication and training can help ease these concerns. Involving teams in the planning process also builds support.

Migration Complexity

Modernizing legacy code is not simple. Legacy systems often have large, tightly coupled codebases. This makes refactoring a big challenge. Data migration is also risky. It is important to maintain data integrity and ensure that no information is lost.

- **Example:** Migrating a legacy ERP system to a cloud platform requires careful planning. Every step must be tested to avoid errors.

- **Solution:** Use proven migration patterns such as the Strangler Fig pattern. This allows you to replace parts of the system gradually rather than all at once.

Ensuring System Availability During Migration

Downtime during the migration can hurt business operations. Modernization must be done in stages to keep systems running.

- **Example:** Transitioning from a monolithic system to microservices may require running both systems in parallel for a time.

- **Solution:** A hybrid approach, where the old and new systems operate together, can minimize disruption. This requires detailed planning and coordination.

Compliance and Regulatory Issues

New regulations must be followed during modernization. Legacy systems might not meet current standards for data protection and privacy. Moving to a new system means rethinking how data is stored and secured.

- **Example:** When migrating data from an old system to the cloud, companies must ensure adherence with GDPR or HIPAA.

- **Solution:** Work with legal and IT experts during the planning phase. Ensure that the new system is built with compliance in mind from the start.

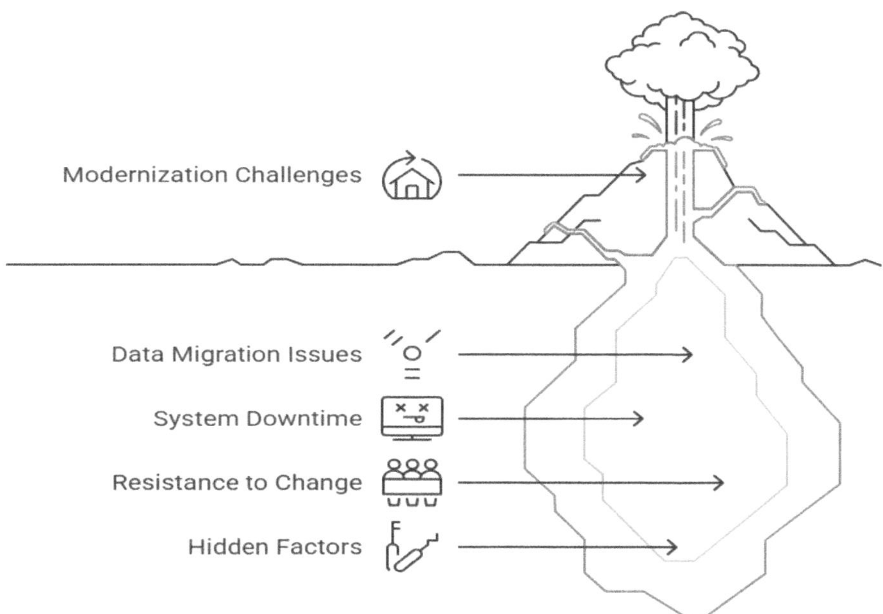

Figure 1-2. *A Visual Representation of Common Modernization Challenges, such as Data Migration Issues, System Downtime, and Resistance to Change*

Choosing the Right Technology Stack

Selecting the right technology stack is a key step in modernization. The stack is a combination of tools and platforms that support the application. The right choices affect performance, security, and future growth.

Technology Stack Overview

When picking a technology stack, consider these factors:

- **Type of Legacy System:** Is it an ERP, CRM, or another internal tool?

- **Business Objectives:** Do you need scalability, AI integration, or mobile accessibility?

- **Developer Skill Sets:** What tools and languages are your teams comfortable with?

Below is an example table of a modern technology stack:

LayerTechnology	
Backend	Spring Boot (for microservices)
Frontend	React (for modern UI)
Middleware	Node.js (for APIs and communication)
Database	PostgreSQL/MongoDB (for structured vs. unstructured data)
Infrastructure	Docker and Kubernetes (for containerization)
Cloud Deployment	Cloud-agnostic (AWS, Azure, GCP)
AI Services	Cloud-based AI (for automation and insights)

Why These Choices?

- **Spring Boot** simplifies microservices development. It allows developers to build independent, small services quickly.

- **React** offers a modern, responsive user interface. It uses reusable components that speed up development.

- **Node.js** helps create fast and efficient APIs. It connects different parts of the application with ease.

- **Docker and Kubernetes** provide a scalable and efficient way to manage resources. They make it easier to deploy applications across various environments.

- **Cloud-based AI** services offer advanced features like predictive analytics. These services do not need on-prem hardware, reducing costs and complexity.

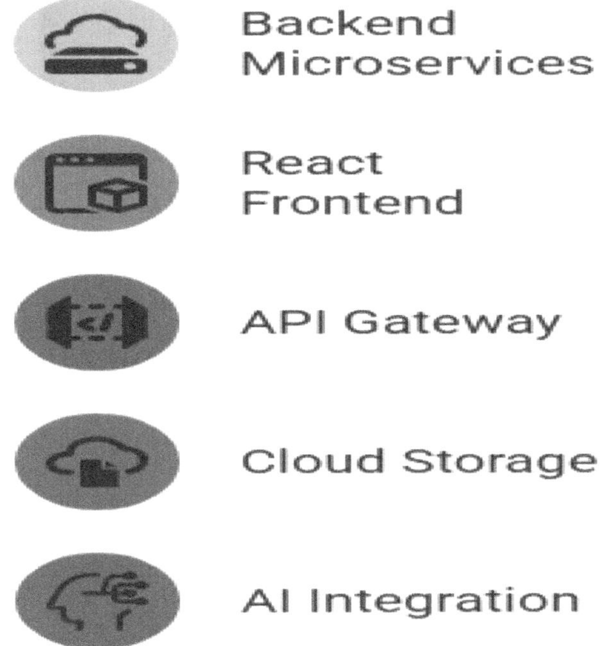

Figure 1-3. *A High-Level Architecture Diagram Showing Backend Microservices, React Frontend, the API Gateway, Cloud Storage, and AI Integration*

Building a Modernization Roadmap

A clear roadmap is vital for a successful modernization project. The roadmap is a detailed plan that guides every step of the journey. It helps teams stay organized and focused. Here is a step-by-step guide for building a modernization roadmap:

Assessment and Planning

- **Identify Modernization Goals:**

  Decide what you want to achieve. This may include cloud migration, better security, or improved performance.

- **Analyze Current System Limitations:**

  Look at the legacy system. Find out what is working and what is not.

- **Prioritize Features for Refactoring:**

  Decide which parts of the application need the most attention. Focus on areas that will bring the biggest benefits when modernized.

Technology Selection

- **Choose Appropriate Tools:**

  Select the best backend, frontend, database, and cloud technologies. Base your decision on business needs and team skills.

- **Decide on a Migration Strategy:**

  Consider whether to lift-and-shift the current system or to refactor and rebuild it. The strategy must suit the current state of the legacy application.

Incremental Migration (Strangler Fig Pattern)

- **Gradual Transition:**

  Instead of rewriting the entire system at once, update it in small steps. This is known as the Strangler Fig pattern.

- **Test Each Component:**

  As you move parts of the system to a modern architecture, test them thoroughly. This helps prevent problems and ensures smooth integration.

Deployment and Optimization

- **Set Up CI/CD Pipelines:**

  Use automation to deploy changes quickly and safely. Continuous integration and deployment help maintain a steady flow of updates.

- **Monitor Application Performance:**

  Keep an eye on the new system. Use monitoring tools to track performance and catch issues early.

- **Iterate and Improve:**

  Modernization is an ongoing process. Keep refining and optimizing the system based on feedback and new business needs.

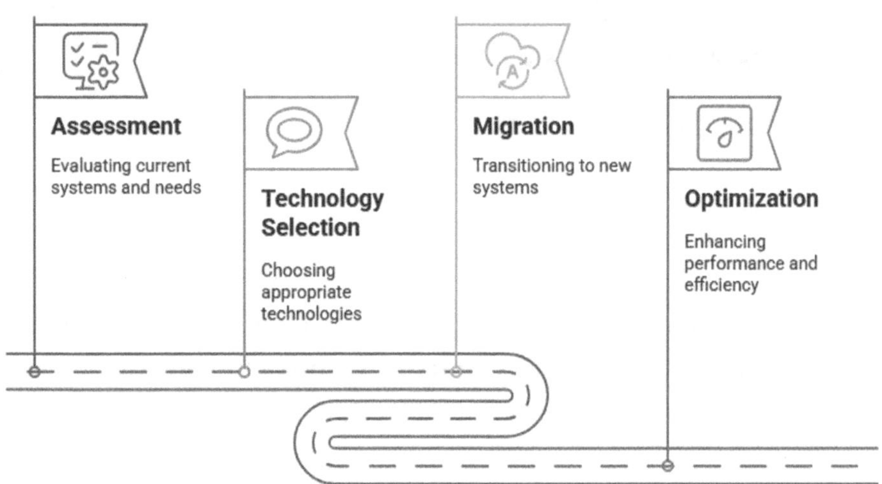

Figure 1-4. A Phased Diagram Showing Assessment, Technology Selection, Migration, and Optimization. Each Phase Builds on the Previous One

Conclusion

Modernizing legacy applications is a crucial step for businesses. It helps companies stay competitive and grow in a fast-changing market. By moving away from monolithic architectures and embracing microservices, cloud infrastructure, and modern integration methods, organizations can build systems that are faster, safer, and more scalable.

This chapter has explained what application modernization is and why it is needed. We looked at the main reasons why legacy applications become obsolete. The challenges of tightly coupled code, high maintenance costs, limited integration, and security risks were discussed. We also reviewed the many benefits, such as improved scalability, reduced costs, faster deployment, seamless integration with new technologies, and enhanced security.

Choosing the right technology stack is another key step. A modern stack, with tools like Spring Boot, React, Node.js, Docker, and cloud-based services, makes it easier to build a resilient application. The roadmap for modernization, including assessment, technology selection, incremental migration, and deployment, provides a clear path forward.

Modernization is not a one-time event. It is a continuous journey. Companies must keep updating their systems to meet new challenges. This ensures they remain competitive and can serve their customers well. With careful planning, clear communication, and the right tools, even complex modernization projects can be successful.

In summary, application modernization is essential for a business's survival and growth. It turns old, inflexible systems into agile, efficient solutions. This chapter has laid the foundation by explaining the need, benefits, challenges, technology choices, and roadmap required for modernization. The journey may be challenging, but the rewards are significant. Companies that modernize can enjoy lower costs, better performance, and the flexibility to embrace new technologies like AI and cloud computing. By following a clear plan, organizations can transform their legacy systems into future-proof assets that drive innovation and business success.

CHAPTER 2

Understanding Legacy Systems

What Are Legacy Systems?

The definition of "legacy system" describes past-generation technology frameworks in which businesses operate today even though they have outlived their original usefulness. It's crucial to understand that these systems, while successful in their time, now hinder business advancement and technological progress. The need for modernization is urgent. Organizations constructed their systems during earlier technological eras and usually fail to deliver adaptable features, scalable characteristics, and modern software and cloud platform interoperability.

The uptake of monolithic systems architecture by legacy systems creates significant challenges for implementer teams who want to expand or change their solutions. Using dated programming languages and outmoded hardware elevates service and protection concerns while driving up support costs. Every organization that depends on outdated systems encounters difficulties when integrating modern tools, performing at optimal levels, and maintaining industry standards. Understanding these challenges is crucial for all involved.

© Mrinmoy Aich and Diganta Sengupta 2026
M. Aich and D. Sengupta, *Cloud-Native Modernization Unleashed,*
https://doi.org/10.1007/979-8-8688-2379-4_2

Examples of legacy systems include

- **On-premise ERP Systems** developed in COBOL or older Java frameworks.

  Large businesses continue operating their enterprise resource planning (ERP) systems developed decades ago using the COBOL programming language or older Java software versions. These systems maintain essential business functions that handle finance operations, supply chain management, and human resource operations. These systems demonstrate limited flexibility, although they are challenging to combine with cloud-based systems and need expert technicians for ongoing support.

- **Traditional CRM Applications** with rigid architectures and no API support.

  In the past, organizations built their customer relationship management (CRM) applications as standalone systems, which provided minimal customization capabilities. Modern CRM tools connect with different marketing systems and cloud analytics databases using APIs. However, legacy systems do not have this capability, so businesses experience challenges when trying to automate customer contact and extract meaningful data insights from their customer information.

- **Custom-built Business Applications** designed for a specific workflow but unable to scale.

  Particular business enterprises have created customized applications specifically for their unique operational sequences. Evolutionary business requirements usually outpace the capabilities of these systems, although they initially provided good results. These systems become problems for innovation and digital transformation because they lack necessary support for scalability, cloud adoption, and mobile accessibility.

Why Do Businesses Still Use Legacy Systems?

The problems that legacy applications create do not stop organizations from preserving them. Businesses typically keep operating legacy systems because of multiple practical needs, financial obligations, and ongoing operational requirements. These are the principal motivations that make companies postpone their aging system updates:

1. **Business Dependency:** Most legacy applications function as vital components for controlling essential business operations like financial management, human resources operations, supply chain operations, and customer connection management. Organizations implanted their business processes on these systems during several years of operation. The replacement process could interrupt business operations, causing workflow delays and possibly leading to revenue reduction and operational productivity problems.

   The banking institution maintains its core banking system functioning on a COBOL-based platform from previous times. Over many years, this outdated system has continued to complete millions of daily transactions. This reliability is a key reason why many organizations choose to keep using legacy systems, despite the potential for complex service interruptions when switching to new, modern solutions.

2. **High Replacement Costs:** Businesses need to spend substantial funds while shifting from old systems to new modern applications. Companies must spend on:

    The purchase of new software development and the licensing of modern solutions plans.

    Employee training and change management.

    Upgrading infrastructure involves moving from on-premise to cloud systems and buying new hardware.

    Finishing modernization projects can take multiple years or lengthy months. Identifying the immediate proof of ROI during the migration process is challenging for organizations because their legacy systems work well enough to delay essential transitions.

3. **Complex Customizations:** Legacy systems require extensive customization to fit specific company business requirements. Over the years, organizations have built custom workflows and business logic and performed numerous integrations that will be hard to duplicate in off-the-shelf modern software tools.

    A manufacturing company operates with a production tracking system built specifically for it, which connects with its current ERP. Moving to new systems would necessitate organizations rebuilding significant custom developments or potentially losing data since businesses need to be apprehensive about system changes.

4. **Data Lock-in:** All businesses collect enormous amounts of data throughout their operation period, which remains deeply contained within their legacy system infrastructure. This data is not just a challenge to migrate but a unique asset that organizations need to manage carefully. Transferring business operations to modern platforms demands extensive work on extracting and transforming legacy data while conducting validation checks, which becomes a complex procedure that takes too much time.

    Current legacy platforms utilize unique data formats that work only with former applications due to technical incompatibilities. Organizations experience concerns about data loss, data corruption, and noncompliance risks when performing a migration. A standard patient records database healthcare provider's use represents a migration hurdle since it lacks current interoperability features while posing technical and compliance issues.

    Companies maintain the use of legacy systems primarily because of their high costs, complex structures, and essential business operational needs. However, increasing threats such as [specific threats] and modern technological advancements like [specific technological advancements] demand that organizations adopt a step-by-step method to transform their legacy applications without interrupting critical business operations.

Common Types of Legacy Architectures

Before diving into the task of application modernization, it's essential to gain a comprehensive understanding of various legacy architectures and their functionalities. These older systems, designed with logical architectural patterns, now present challenges to scalability, maintenance needs, and integration requirements. By arming yourself with this knowledge, you'll be better prepared to navigate the complexities of modernization.

Monolithic Architecture

Monolithic architecture, a system with a single, large code structure connecting all application modules, presents significant challenges. The lack of independence between components makes independent modification and scaling efforts difficult. This packaging of the application into one unit hinders the system's adaptability and scalability.

- A **single, unified codebase** where all application modules (UI, business logic, database) are tightly coupled.

  The overall codebase contains all application modules together as a unified package.

  The system needs to reinstall the complete application even if an operator changes only a small portion of the system.

- Changes in one part of the application often require redeploying the entire system.

When scaling, the whole system becomes less efficient because it requires all components to scale together, although only a single component needs additional resources.

Debugging procedures and maintenance tasks become intricate because errors affecting any part of the application result in system-wide consequences.

- **Example:** The ERP system contains three functions: inventory management, finance, and CRM within a single integrated codebase. When the company wishes to enhance CRM capabilities, it needs to transform and redeploy all sections of the ERP system, thus prolonging development periods and multiplying failure risks. The following section will explain the architecture of monolithic systems and also discuss the challenges.

Modernization Path Forward

While traditional monolithic systems have served businesses well for many years, they now pose obstacles to scaling and maintaining software codebases, as well as embracing cloud deployment. However, the path to modernization offers a promising future. Enterprises that embrace microservices or cloud-native adoption as part of their transformation strategy can expect to achieve better system flexibility and performance, ushering in a new era of efficiency and innovation.

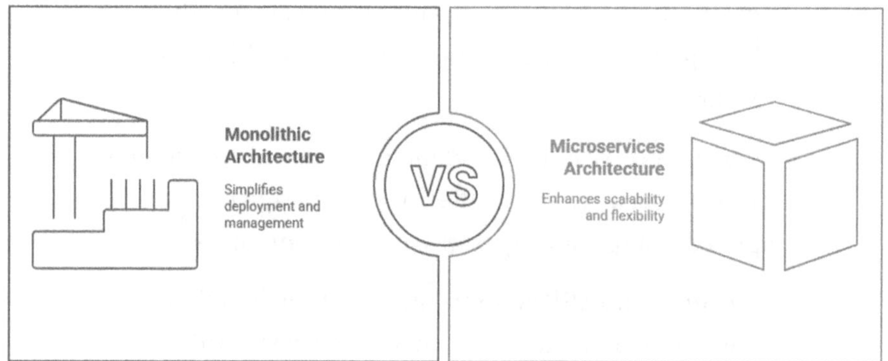

Figure 2-1. Monolithic Architecture Example (A diagram showing a single large block representing a monolithic system with tightly coupled components)

Layered Architecture (N-Tier Applications)

Applications achieve logical division of functions through layered architecture implementations that implement N-tier techniques for separating program elements. This design approach makes the application easier to handle because it breaks down functions into separate modules that facilitate more manageable updates. This architectural design requires all layers to depend on each other, thus making maintenance and expansion challenging.

- **Key Characteristics:**

   The system function operates through multiple levels of operation, which typically establish this sequence: User interface operations from the presentation layer control screen are displayed to transmit information to end-users. The system performs business operations inside this layer while it carries out rule-based data processing. Data access layer: Manages communication with the database and external data sources. The database is the single source for storing and extracting information data directly. Requests initiated at the user interface layer must pass through each successive layer, starting with business logic and moving to the database before execution. Although dependent systems disrupt system modification, the modular structure enables developers to maintain structured work methods during development and testing.

- **Example:**

Consider a 3-tier e-commerce system where: The presentation layer serves customers by means of its graphical user interface for online product search activities. The API in the business logic layer processes orders through the discount application. The database layer contains customer data jointly with inventory details stored in either MySQL or PostgreSQL relational databases. AI-enabled product recommendation deployment proves challenging for the business because the current system does not support suitable integration of machine learning models. Updating the layers produces complex dependencies with other layers, thus slowing down development speed.

N-Tier Architecture

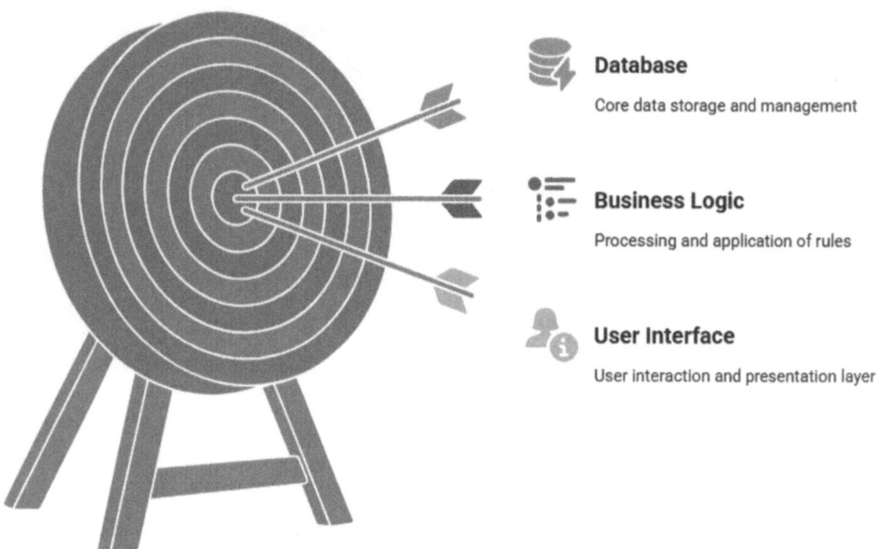

Figure 2-2. N-Tier Architecture (A diagram displaying three layers: UI, Business Logic, and Database, connected vertically.)

Service-Oriented Architecture (SOA)

Service-Oriented Architecture (SOA) represents an application design methodology that divides information systems into independent network-operating service systems. SOA provides service reuse, flexibility, and scalability through functional service capabilities but differs from monolithic and layered architectures that support tight component connections.

- **Key Characteristics:**

    Service operations remain autonomous, and developers can create services individually before deploying and updating them.

Two services establish their connection through network protocols, including HTTP and SOAP.

Service requests get managed through an Enterprise Service Bus (ESB) to achieve quick and efficient communication between diverse services.

SOAP-based web services define the basis for application communication thanks to WSDL (Web Services Description Language).

Service reuse becomes possible through this methodology, which cuts down development expenses and project durations.

- **Example:**

Different financial operations are handled through multiple autonomous banking services within a contemporary banking system, which operate as follows:

Account Services operates as an independent service unit that manages user profiles, transactions, and account balance records.

This service coordinates between application handling, approvals, and loan payment transactions.

The customer management service maintains customer records and preferences while storing support cases.

The individual banking services function independently by exchanging information through an Enterprise Service Bus (ESB). Customer loan applications require the loan processing service to contact account services for fee checks and customer management for verifying identity details. These services utilize the ESB to transmit requests instead of establishing direct hardcoded connections, guaranteeing flexible and modular operations.

Challenges and Considerations

Adopting service-oriented architecture enhances service reuse and produces better modularity but introduces certain user restrictions.

SOAP-based web services and ESB create performance delays because they operate slower than simpler RESTful APIs.

Multiple service management remains complex because strong governance policies and dedicated API management tools are needed to maintain and secure the services.

Various organizations that discontinue using SOA patterns shift toward microservices architecture because it delivers superior adaptability.

Next Steps

Businesses operating with SOA-based applications need to consider upgrading their infrastructure by moving from SOAP-based services to RESTful APIs and integrating cloud-native services with microservices implementation for higher operating speed and adaptability.

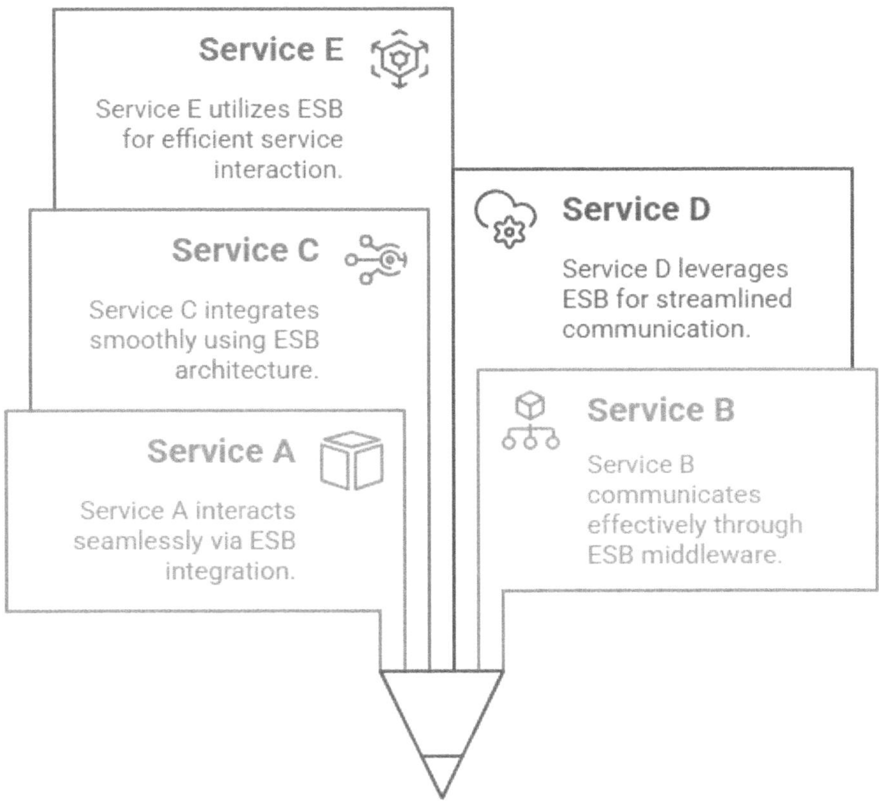

Figure 2-3. SOA Architecture (A diagram showing multiple services communicating through an ESB.)

Challenges of Legacy Systems

Scalability Issues

- Monolithic applications do not scale efficiently; even minor performance improvements require **scaling the entire system**.

- In contrast, microservices allow scaling of individual components as needed.

Maintenance Overhead

- Legacy systems often use outdated programming languages (e.g., COBOL, VB6, early Java versions).

- Finding developers with expertise in these languages is becoming increasingly difficult.

Integration Limitations

- Older applications do not support **RESTful APIs**, making integration with modern services (AI, cloud-based analytics, third-party APIs) difficult.

- Modernization requires introducing **API gateways** to expose functionalities securely.

Example

A legacy **on-premise CRM system** may store customer data in an **SQL Server database**, but it lacks APIs to share data with cloud-based marketing tools.

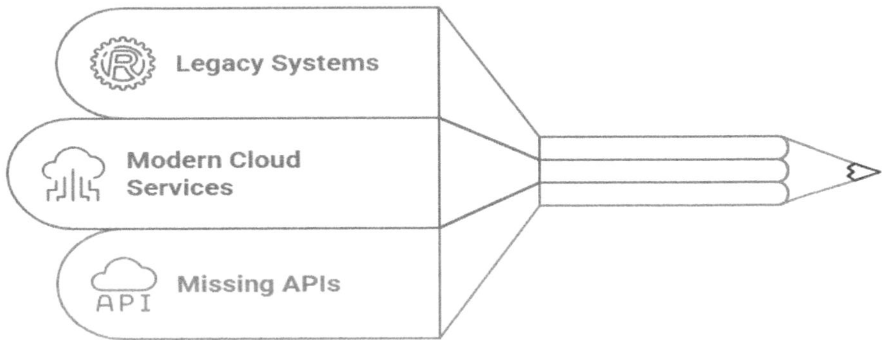

Figure 2-4. Legacy System Integration Challenges (A diagram showing an old system failing to connect with modern cloud services due to missing APIs.)

Security and Compliance Risks

- Older systems often lack **regular security patches**, making them vulnerable to cyber threats.

- Many legacy applications do not comply with modern regulations like **GDPR** and **HIPAA**.

Identifying the Right Modernization Strategy

To modernize a legacy system, we must first analyze:

- **Current limitations and bottlenecks** (performance, security, integration).

- **Business priorities** (cost reduction, scalability, new feature enablement).

- **Technology feasibility** (available modernization paths).

Key Modernization Strategies

Modernization Approach	Description	Effort Required	Business Impact
Lift-and-Shift	Move the legacy system to the cloud without code changes.	Low	Minimal, mostly cost savings.
Replatforming	Migrate with minor modifications (e.g., switch database, containerize app).	Medium	Improved performance, some scalability.
Refactoring	Rewriting parts of the application to use modern architectures (e.g., microservices).	High	High flexibility, better scalability.
Rebuilding	Completely redesigning the application from scratch.	Very High	Maximum agility, new business opportunities.

Explanation of Terms

- **Lift-and-Shift**: This strategy involves moving existing applications to the cloud with minimal changes, retaining the original architecture and codebase.

- **Replatforming**: This approach involves making some changes to the application during migration, such as changing the database or using containers, to improve performance and scalability without a complete overhaul.

- **Refactoring**: This strategy entails modifying the existing code to improve its structure and efficiency, typically by adopting modern development practices like microservices architecture.

- **Rebuilding**: This is the most intensive strategy, where the application is completely redesigned and built anew, allowing for the incorporation of the latest technologies and best practices for maximum operational agility.

Figure 2-5. Modernization Approaches *(A diagram comparing the four strategies with cost and complexity considerations.)*

Choosing the Best Approach

- If a system is **stable but costly**, a **Lift-and-Shift** to the cloud might be best.

- If **performance and flexibility** are critical, **Refactoring or Rebuilding** is preferred.

- If the system has **modular components**, a **Hybrid Approach** (combining replatforming and refactoring) can be beneficial.

Preparing for Modernization

Conducting a Legacy System Assessment

- Identify **high-risk dependencies** (e.g., legacy databases, hard-coded business rules).

- Analyze **code maintainability** and **security risks**.

- Evaluate **data integrity** (migrations must preserve business data).

Establishing a Modernization Roadmap

Application modernization is a sophisticated process in which defined logistics frameworks serve as the foundation for successfully transforming organizations into contemporary and adaptable system architectures. Make a sound plan to decrease risks and achieve maximum business worth while maintaining operational continuity. A comprehensive modernization roadmap consists of the following steps that organizations can adopt.

Discovery and Planning

Any modernization effort requires organizations to start by evaluating their existing system and defining the business goal and technical requirement.

- Organizations should locate the core issues in their current applications by assessing performance problems, security threats, and integration breakdowns.

- Business leaders should assess modernization's effects while establishing prioritization levels to move crucial applications.

- Organizations must examine potential safety hazards, particularly data loss, downtime, and standard compatibility challenges.

- A thorough strategic plan must describe project timelines and budget allocations while listing all involved stakeholders.

Example:

A financial services company initiates its payment processing system modernization by examining the boundaries between systems. Then, it evaluates security needs and cloud readiness to determine a migration approach that will be implemented gradually.

Technology Selection

Organizations need to make the right technology decisions as they determine the success of their modernization project. The objective involves selecting current-day frameworks that deliver scalability and integration abilities with performance enhancement. Organizations must select:

- Organizations can choose from three backend system options: Spring Boot, Node.js, and .NET Core.

- Frontend technologies: React, Angular, Vue.js.

- Cloud platforms: AWS, Azure, Google Cloud.

- Containerization and orchestration: Docker, Kubernetes.

- Databases: NoSQL (MongoDB, DynamoDB) and modern SQL (PostgreSQL, MySQL).

Example:

By converting a legacy Java EE application, developers can achieve better scalability through Spring Boot migration, which creates microservice architecture. Both frontend modules can benefit from a modernization project with Angular or React to achieve superior user experiences.

Incremental Migration

Businesses choosing the Strangler Fig Pattern can pursue segmental migrations through an incremental approach. The new services can step in through gradual replacement until old services are substituted successfully without interrupting complete system functions.

- The first step requires assessing modularizable product parts such as authentication methods and reporting systems.

- Implementing new services must co-occur with the current system until new services fulfill their purpose.

- The process of shifting obsolete components to retiring functions completes new operational capabilities.

Example:

An e-commerce enterprise starting to move away from a monolithic order management system should convert the inventory management function into a microservice before moving toward other sections, including order tracking and payment processing.

Testing and Validation

Strict testing protocols verify the stability, efficiency, and security of the new environment after migration initiation. Key testing processes include

- The new system must be tested to verify its expected behavior during functional testing.

- **Security Testing:** Identify vulnerabilities before deployment.

- **Performance Testing:** Verify scalability under different workloads.

- Organizations must validate data to ensure precise migration of all information with full accessibility.

Example:

A logistics company performs load testing on its tracking system migration to the cloud to verify its capability of handling peak demand requirements.

Deployment and Optimization

The deployment of the modernized system begins with implementing CI/CD pipelines to achieve automated and smooth updates. The deployed system requires continuous observation through optimization techniques that drive performance growth and cost performance improvements.

- Implementing CI/CD systems should include automated features for code deployment and testing functionality.

- The organization should adjust its cloud resources according to changing demand patterns.

- **Monitor System Health:** Use tools like Prometheus and Grafana for real-time tracking.

Example:

Implementing a contemporary patient management system through a Kubernetes deployment provides system auto-scaling features and CI/CD pipelines for continuous software updates.

A detailed modernization strategy guides organizations through a break-free transition from traditional systems to contemporary cloud-based applications. Organizations that develop their applications through a step-based process from planning through deployment minimize risks, achieve performance goals, and protect their future needs.

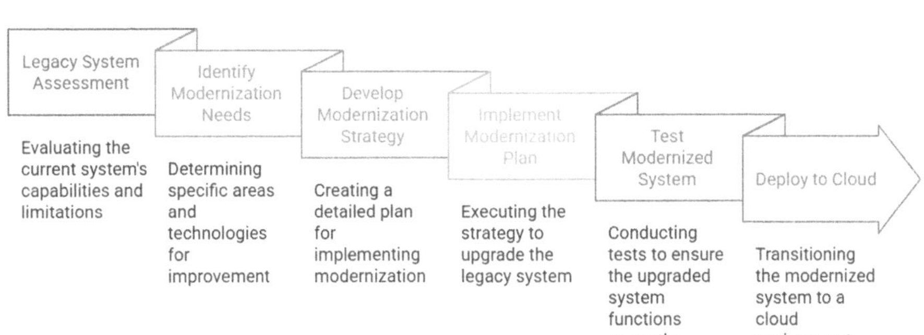

Figure 2-6. Modernization Roadmap (A step-by-step flowchart showing the journey from legacy assessment to cloud deployment.)

Conclusion

Any successful initiative for application modernization requires a complete understanding of legacy systems as its initial base. Systems that emerged earlier continue to create difficulties regarding scalability and security concerns, integration problems, and high maintenance costs. The business risks declining performance against competitors whose infrastructure uses up-to-date cloud-native systems and contemporary technology.

An organization can discover its legacy system structural limitations by detecting standard architectures, including monolithic systems, layered (N-tier) architectures, and service-oriented architectures (SOA). Businesses can develop strategic modernization strategies by identifying system constraints rather than making extensive replacement attempts.

Modern platforms receive a seamless transition from legacy systems when organizations define clear plans for modernization. A systematic discovery and planning process, technology selection, including rental migration testing, and deployment enable companies to decrease dangers and increase operational efficiency. Through implementations of Spring Boot Kubernetes microservices with cloud computing organizations, they experience better scalability, operational price reduction, and enhanced flexibility and performance capabilities.

Application modernization represents a full-scale business transformation beyond standard technical modernization. Entire organizations advance innovation rates, quicken development timelines, and build superior customer interactions through modernization adoption. Organizations that maintain technological innovation will secure enduring development, enhanced protection, and market leadership in the continuous digital environment.

CHAPTER 3

Designing a Modern Cloud-Native Architecture

Introduction to Cloud-Native Architecture

We discussed the challenges of legacy systems and various modernization methods in the previous chapter. Now, we delve into the design of contemporary cloud-native architectural solutions, which are poised to replace and extend existing legacy programs. Cloud-native architecture, a fundamental framework, is designed to create scalable, flexible, and high-performance applications that fully harness the power of cloud infrastructure, ensuring efficient operations.

What Is Cloud-Native Architecture?

The specifications of cloud-native architecture are engineered to extract complete advantages from cloud computing platforms through automatic scalability and ongoing availability features. Cloud-native systems directly interact with cloud platforms by utilizing all their available features instead of traditional ones targeting on-premise environments.

© Mrinmoy Aich and Diganta Sengupta 2026
M. Aich and D. Sengupta, *Cloud-Native Modernization Unleashed,*
https://doi.org/10.1007/979-8-8688-2379-4_3

A cloud-native architecture consists of the following main characteristics:

- Applications under this design principle are divided into miniature independent services that serve individual tasks. Each service becomes upgradeable and scales independently because of this approach.

- Containerization and orchestration combine packages that deploy self-contained applications with their necessary components between multiple operational settings. Orchestration, which is the automated arrangement, coordination, and management of complex computer systems, is a key aspect of cloud-native architecture. With Kubernetes orchestration tools, clients achieve automated management of resource scaling and distribution and scaling operations.

- Cloud-native applications allow scale-on-demand operations as well as automated development processes. The infrastructure provides self-healing abilities, which means that in the event of a failure, the system can automatically detect and correct the issue without human intervention, thereby enhancing resilience. Automation tools further decrease human interaction for better efficiency.

- Organizations stand to gain a multitude of benefits when they leverage cloud-native architecture to develop adaptable, scalable, and cost-effective applications that can swiftly accommodate rapid business needs. We will now explore the individual components and best practices for creating effective cloud-native systems in the upcoming parts of this discussion, instilling confidence in the adaptability of this architecture.

Figure 3-1. Traditional vs. Cloud-Native Architecture (*A side-by-side comparison of a monolithic system vs. microservices deployed in containers, managed via Kubernetes.*)

Transitioning from Monolithic to Microservices

Why Microservices?

- **Scalability:** Scale individual services based on demand.

- **Flexibility:** Different services can be developed in different technologies.

- **Resilience:** A failure in one service does not impact others.

- **Faster Development:** Small, independent teams can develop and deploy services.

Breaking Down a Monolithic System

Instead of migrating everything at once, we follow a **Strangler Fig pattern**, where we gradually replace legacy modules with microservices.

Example:

Consider a legacy ERP system managing:

- **Order Processing**
- **Inventory Management**
- **Billing and Payments**

We can split these into microservices as follows:

1. **Order Service:** Handles order creation and tracking.

2. **Inventory Service:** Manages stock levels and product availability.

3. **Billing Service**: Processes payments and invoices.

    Pitfalls: Moving away from the monolith system to a collection of smaller microservices has its own set of headaches:

    Data Consistency: Imagine each system has its own separate notebook for keeping records. If a customer updates their address in the "Orders" system, how does the "Shipping" system find out? Keeping the data in sync across all these separate notebooks without creating conflicts is a major challenge.

    Distributed Transactions: What if a single customer action requires multiple systems to do something? For example, placing an order might involve the "Inventory" system, the "Payments" system, and the "Shipping" system. If the payment fails, you have to make sure the inventory is "put back" and the shipment is cancelled. Coordinating a single, all-or-nothing transaction across these separate services is incredibly complex.

    Service Discovery: When you have dozens or even hundreds of little systems, how do they find each other? If the "Orders" system needs to talk to the "Inventory" system, it needs to know its exact location (address). But what if that location changes? You need a reliable "address book" (service discovery) that's always up to date so the services can communicate.

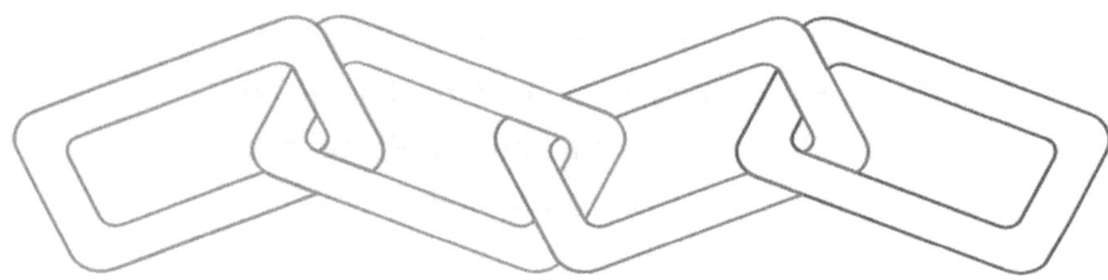

Figure 3-2. Transition from Monolithic to Microservices (A monolithic ERP system being split into microservices, each communicating via REST APIs.)

Choosing the Right Technology Stack

Backend—Spring Boot and Node.js

- **Spring Boot:** Ideal for microservices due to its lightweight architecture and built-in support for RESTful APIs.

- **Node.js:** Used for real-time applications and asynchronous processing.

Frontend—React

- React enables fast, interactive, and reusable UI components.

- Works well with **REST APIs** and **GraphQL** for dynamic data fetching.

Database—Polyglot Persistence

Each microservice can use the most suitable database type:

- **SQL (PostgreSQL, MySQL):** Used for transactional data (Billing, Orders).

- **NoSQL (MongoDB, DynamoDB):** Ideal for flexible data models (Inventory, User Preferences).

- **In-Memory Databases (Redis, Memcached):** Used for caching frequently accessed data.

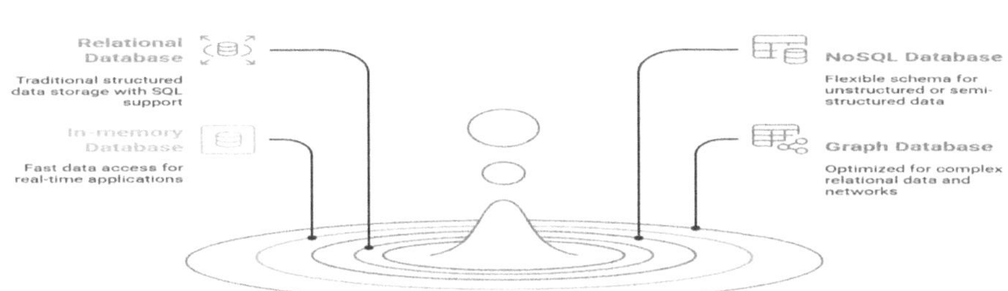

Figure 3-3. Microservices with Different Databases (Diagram showing microservices connected to different types of databases.)

Designing API Communication Between Microservices

Microservices interact using APIs. We can choose between:

REST APIs

- Simple and widely used.

- Stateless communication between services.

- **Example**: `GET/orders/123` retrieves order details.

GraphQL APIs

- Efficient querying, fetching only required data.

- **Example**: A React frontend requests only "Order ID" and "Total Price" instead of the full order details.

Event-Driven Architecture with Kafka/RabbitMQ

Instead of RESTful synchronous calls, services communicate asynchronously using **events**.

- **Example**: When an order is placed, the **Order Service** sends an event to Kafka.

- The **Inventory Service** listens to the event and updates stock levels.

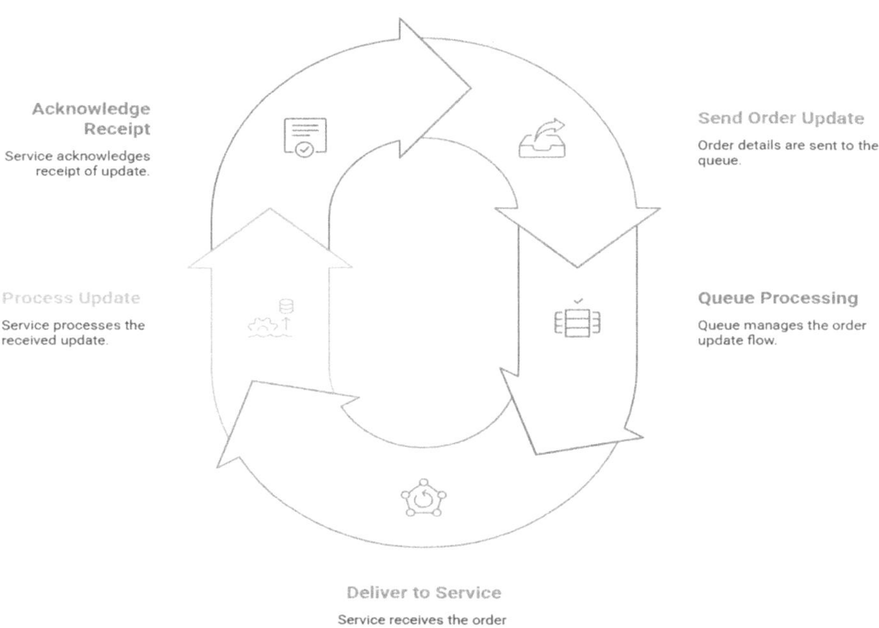

Figure 3-4. **Event-Driven Communication in Microservices** *(A message queue passing order updates between microservices asynchronously.)*

Deployment Model	Description	Example Providers
IaaS (Infrastructure-as-a-Service)	Provides virtual machines, storage, and networking.	AWS EC2, Google Compute Engine, Azure Virtual Machines
PaaS (Platform-as-a-Service)	Fully managed environments for app deployment.	AWS Elastic Beanstalk, Google App Engine, Azure App Service
Serverless (FaaS—Function-as-a-Service)	Runs code without managing servers.	AWS Lambda, Google Cloud Functions, Azure Functions

Deploying the Application on a Cloud Infrastructure

Explanation of Terms

- **IaaS (Infrastructure-as-a-Service)**: Offers fundamental computing resources such as virtual machines and storage, allowing users to manage their own applications and operating systems.

- **PaaS (Platform-as-a-Service)**: Provides a platform allowing developers to build, deploy, and manage applications without worrying about the underlying infrastructure, streamlining the development process.

- **Serverless (FaaS—Function-as-a-Service)**: Enables developers to run code in response to events without managing servers, allowing for automatic scaling and more efficient resource utilization.

Containerization with Docker

- Each microservice is packaged as a **Docker container**, ensuring consistency across environments.

- Example Dockerfile for Spring Boot microservice:

```dockerfile
dockerfile
CopyEdit
FROM openjdk:17
COPY target/order-service.jar /app/order-service.jar
ENTRYPOINT ["java", "-jar", "/app/order-service.jar"]
```

Container Orchestration with Kubernetes

- Kubernetes **manages multiple containers**, ensuring:

  - **Auto-scaling** based on traffic.

  - **Load balancing** between instances.

  - **Self-healing** if a container crashes.

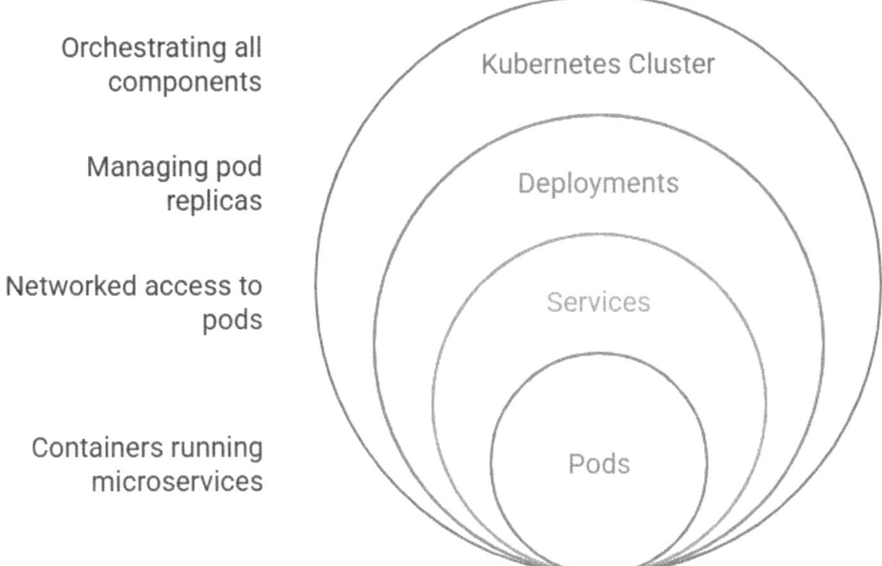

Figure 3-5. Kubernetes Architecture (Diagram showing a Kubernetes cluster with multiple microservices deployed in pods.)

Securing the Application

Security is critical when modernizing applications.

Authentication and Authorization

- Use **OAuth 2.0 and JWT (JSON Web Tokens)** for secure API authentication.

- **Example**: Users log in via an authentication service, receive a JWT, and use it to access microservices.

API Gateway for Security and Rate Limiting

- An **API Gateway** (e.g., Kong, Nginx, AWS API Gateway) handles security policies and limits API requests.

Secure Communication with TLS Encryption

- All microservices should communicate via **HTTPS (TLS encryption)** to prevent data leaks.

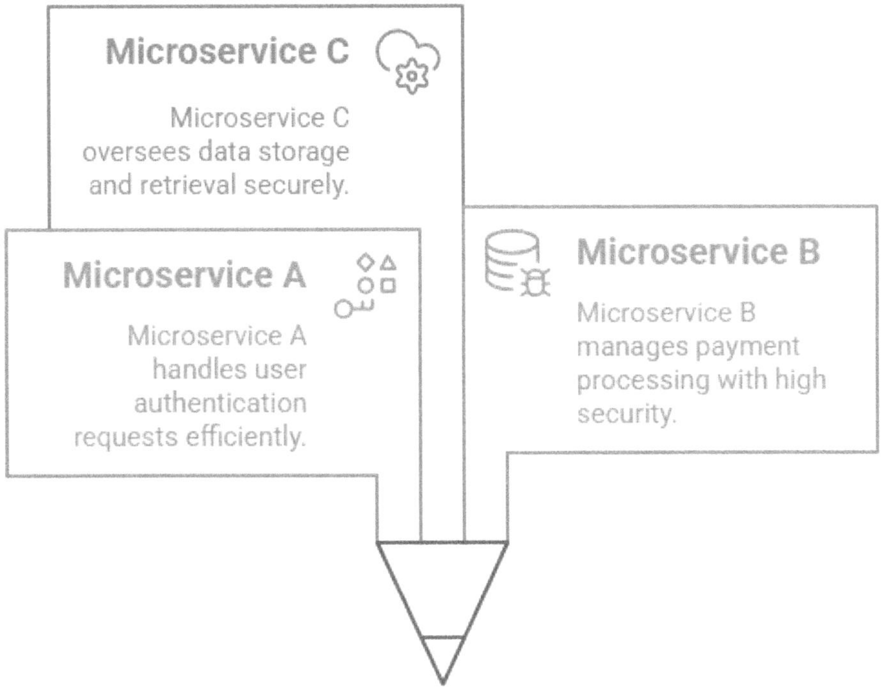

Figure 3-6. Secure API Gateway (Diagram showing microservices behind an API Gateway with authentication and security policies.)

AI Strategy in Modernization

AI can enhance modern applications in several ways:

AI-Powered Chatbots for Customer Support

- Integrate **NLP-based chatbots** (e.g., AWS Lex, Google Dialogflow) for automated responses.

AI-Driven Predictive Analytics

- Use AI to analyze past orders and predict **future demand** in the supply chain.

- **Example**: AI suggests stock replenishment based on sales patterns.

Intelligent Fraud Detection

- AI models detect **suspicious transactions** and alert the fraud prevention team.

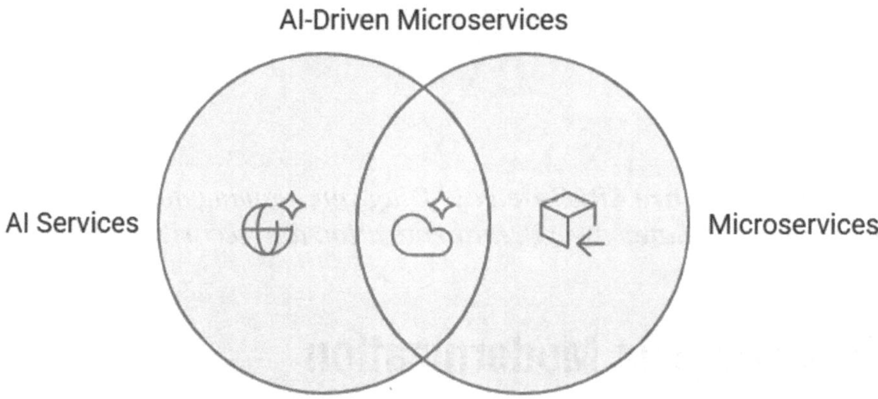

Figure 3-7. AI Services Integrated into Microservices (A microservices diagram showing AI services interacting with customer and inventory systems.)

Conclusion

This section explained the process for converting heritage monolithic systems into cloud-native microservices-based solutions in detail. Every business operating in a competitive market must use contemporary cloud-native solutions to enhance flexibility and efficiency while developing scalable operations.

We established the modernization techniques as our research focus by straightforwardly describing them.

A monolithic application breakdown drives organizations to develop microservices, which involve splitting big, interconnected systems into separate, deployable, independent, autonomous services that allow independent scaling.

Establishing dependable, efficient, scalable cloud-native applications requires selecting an optimum mix of Spring Boot interfaces and running them with Kubernetes Docker, API Gateways, and serverless computing technologies during modernization processes.

The optimal API security steps generate reliable mutual service communication using RESTful APIs and GraphQL alongside OAuth and JWT authentication protocols.

Integrating cloud deployment strategies with Kubernetes orchestration enables our organization to automate CI/CD pipelines and execute container orchestration through cost-effective application management via automated control systems.

When organizations unite AI-powered analytical approaches and automatic systems with wise decision frameworks to improve business applications, they gain enhanced business operations and customer solutions.

Cloud-native architecture allows organizations to merge tools that stop software from aging with technologies for immediate innovation aut, automatic integration, and flexible business solutions. We will study the deployment process of Spring Boot applications built from scratch that utilize Kubernetes containers for deployment.

CHAPTER 4

Implementing Microservices with Spring Boot, Node.js, and React

Introduction

In the last chapter, we analyzed modern cloud-native architecture design procedures, which included microservice partitioning, technology stack selection, and details about security and scalability implementation.

The following part moves from architectural planning to applying practical methods for creating and deploying these cloud-native applications. This chapter will cover

- The implementation of Spring Boot microservices together with Docker will establish our environment.

- Configuring Kubernetes for container orchestration

M. Aich and D. Sengupta, *Cloud-Native Modernization Unleashed,*
https://doi.org/10.1007/979-8-8688-2379-4_4

- A microservice architecture needs API gateways and service discovery mechanisms to achieve efficient microservice communication.

- Distributed cloud environments demand proper implementation of security measures along with compliance features.

- Best practices enable the optimization of both system scalability and performance results.

The final summit of this chapter will grant you thorough expertise in building and managing cloud-native applications using Spring Boot, Kubernetes, and cloud infrastructure.

Now, we will **implement a real-world microservices-based application** using

- **Spring Boot** for backend services

- **Node.js** for event-driven services

- **React** for frontend UI

- **Docker and Kubernetes** for deployment

We will also integrate **API Gateway**, **database connections**, and **messaging systems** to make our system scalable and efficient.

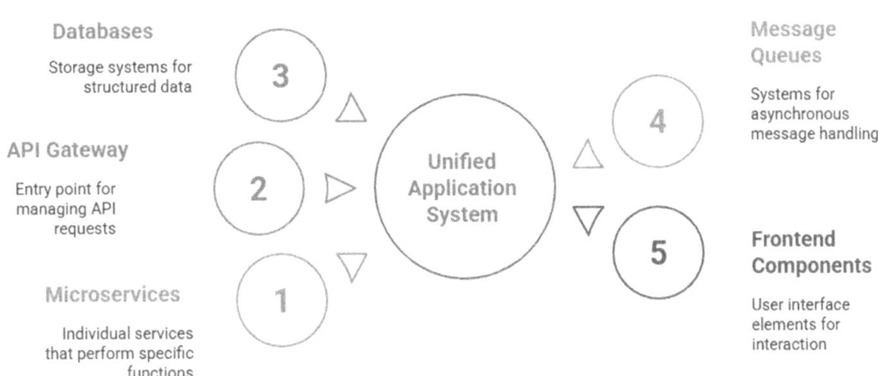

Figure 4-1. *High-Level Architecture of Our Application (Diagram showing microservices, API Gateway, databases, message queues, and frontend components.)*

Microservices Breakdown

Microservices to Be Implemented

The construction of a scalable cloud-native application requires implementing three core microservices. The deployment system splits each microservice to run alone yet connects all services through API standards, enabling best practices for security measures, performance expansion, and system reliability.

User Service

The User Service controls all user management features through its account creation functionality, authentication, and profile editing capabilities. It will be responsible for:

- The application implements JWT authentication and OAuth 2.0 protocols for user authorization procedures.

- The system manages user profiles and stores account details.

- A role-based access control (RBAC) implementation exists to secure the system.

- The system must connect with external identity providers through Google, Facebook, and Okta.

The service utilizes Spring Boot as the framework, Spring Security, the PostgreSQL database, and Redis for session control.

Order Service

Through its functionality, the Order Service performs as an order management system that processes payments and tracks transactions.

- This service enables the real-time creation of new orders along with their maintenance and real-time tracking.

- The application directs all payment processing responsibilities to external payment gateways, including Stripe and PayPal.

- The system enables complete management of orders along with all monetary customer transactions.

- Operations and billing activities remain transactionally sound through distributed event-driven processes.

The order application uses the Spring Boot technology framework, along with Kafka (event streaming), a PostgreSQL database, and the Stripe API for payment integration.

Inventory Service

The Inventory Service controls merchandise inventory amounts together with product availability.

- The system tracks inventory volume and completes stock updates instantly.

- The system will automatically modify stock after customers make purchases through order placement.

- The system should alert other connected services during stock quantity depletion.

- The system should incorporate warehouse management systems to enable automation capabilities.

- The core technology components used for this system are Spring Boot, MySQL, and Kubernetes Horizontal Pod Autoscaler (HPA).

The application architecture uses Docker to package each microservice for Kubernetes management through its RESTful API network, which incorporates Kafka or RabbitMQ as message broker solutions. Service development becomes independent, and deployment happens autonomously because the modular structure boosts scalability, high availability, and fault tolerance.

Service Name	Description	Technology Used
Order Service	Manages orders, tracks order status	Spring Boot, PostgreSQL
Inventory Service	Updates stock levels, checks availability	Spring Boot, MongoDB
Billing Service	Processes payments and invoices	Node.js, Stripe API, MySQL

Deployment Information

Docker containers will deploy each service, with Kubernetes functions as the orchestration system. The deployment architecture enables scalable and efficient microservice management, which makes updates and deployments easy throughout the application.

Setting Up the Order Service (Spring Boot)

Step 1: Creating a New Spring Boot Project

We use **Spring Initializr** to generate a Spring Boot project with the following dependencies:

- **Spring Web** (for REST APIs)

- **Spring Data JPA** (for database interaction)

- **Spring Boot Actuator** (for monitoring)

- **PostgreSQL Driver** (for persistence)

Project Structure

```bash
CopyEdit
order-service/
│── src/main/java/com/example/orderservice/
│   ├── controller/      # Handles API requests
│   ├── service/         # Business logic
│   ├── repository/      # Database interaction
│   ├── model/           # Data models
│   ├── config/          # Configuration files
```

```
|── src/main/resources/
|    ├── application.yml # Configurations
|── pom.xml             # Dependencies
```

Step 2: Defining the Order Entity

Create a Java class to represent an order.

```java
CopyEdit
@Entity
@Table(name = "orders")
public class Order {
    @Id
    @GeneratedValue(strategy = GenerationType.IDENTITY)
    private Long id;
    private String product;
    private int quantity;
    private String status;  // PENDING, SHIPPED, DELIVERED
}
```

Step 3: Creating a REST Controller

The Order Service exposes RESTful APIs to manage orders.

```java
CopyEdit
@RestController
@RequestMapping("/orders")
public class OrderController {

    @Autowired
    private OrderService orderService;
```

```java
@PostMapping
public ResponseEntity<Order> placeOrder(@RequestBody Order
order) {
    return ResponseEntity.ok(orderService.
    createOrder(order));
}

@GetMapping("/{id}")
public ResponseEntity<Order> getOrder(@PathVariable
Long id) {
    return ResponseEntity.ok(orderService.getOrder
    ById(id));
}
}
```

Data Flow from Frontend to Database

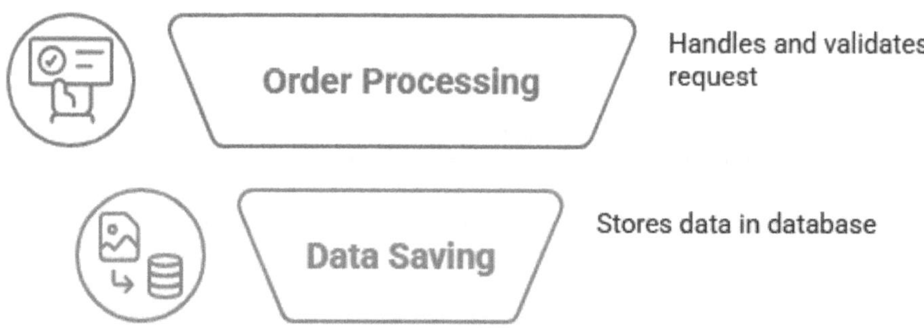

Figure 4-2. API Interaction Between Frontend and Order Service
(The React frontend sends a POST request to Order Service, which processes and saves data in PostgreSQL.)

Setting Up the Inventory Service (Spring Boot and MongoDB)

The Inventory Service will use **MongoDB** for flexible schema storage.

Defining the Inventory Model

```java
CopyEdit
@Document(collection = "inventory")
public class Inventory {
    @Id
    private String id;
    private String productName;
    private int stock;
}
```

Implementing the Inventory API

```java
CopyEdit
@RestController
@RequestMapping("/inventory")
public class InventoryController {

    @Autowired
    private InventoryService inventoryService;

    @GetMapping("/{product}")
    public ResponseEntity<Integer> checkStock(@PathVariable
    String product) {
```

```java
        return ResponseEntity.ok(inventoryService.getStock
        (product));
    }
}
```

Inventory Repository

```java
import org.springframework.data.mongodb.repository.
MongoRepository;

public interface InventoryRepository extends
MongoRepository<Inventory, String> {
    Inventory findByProductName(String productName);
}
```

Inventory Service Interface

```java
public interface InventoryService {
    int getStock(String productName);
    void updateStock(String productName, int newStock);
    Inventory createOrUpdateItem(Inventory item);
}
```

Inventory Service Implementation

```java
import org.springframework.beans.factory.annotation.Autowired;
import org.springframework.stereotype.Service;

@Service
public class InventoryServiceImpl implements InventoryService {

    @Autowired
    private InventoryRepository inventoryRepository;
```

```java
@Override
public int getStock(String productName) {
    Inventory inventory = inventoryRepository.findByProduct
    Name(productName);

    if (inventory == null) {
        return 0; // or throw Exception depending on your
        API design
    }

    return inventory.getStock();
}

@Override
public void updateStock(String productName, int newStock) {
    Inventory inventory = inventoryRepository.findByProduct
    Name(productName);

    if (inventory == null) {
        inventory = new Inventory();
        inventory.setProductName(productName);
    }

    inventory.setStock(newStock);
    inventoryRepository.save(inventory);
}

@Override
public Inventory createOrUpdateItem(Inventory item) {
    Inventory existing = inventoryRepository.
    findByProductName(item.getProductName());

    if (existing != null) {
        item.setId(existing.getId());
```

```
    }

    return inventoryRepository.save(item);
  }
}
```

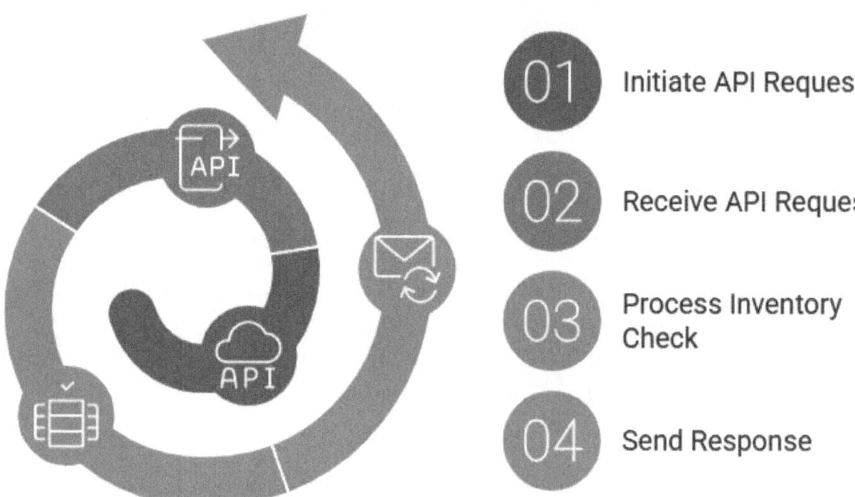

Figure 4-3. Order Service Checking Inventory Before Placing an Order *(Diagram showing API request from Order Service to Inventory Service via REST API.)*

End-to-End Flow (High Level)

1. **Initiate API Request:** Order Service decides it needs to check/lock inventory and sends an HTTP request to Inventory Service.

2. **Receive API Request**: Inventory Service accepts the request (controller layer), validates it, and hands it to the service layer.

3. **Process Inventory Check**: The service layer checks DB (and optionally reserves/locks stock), applies business rules, and persists changes if required.

4. **Send Response**: Inventory Service returns a response with status and payload; Order Service consumes it and proceeds (or handles failures).

Implementing the Billing Service (Node.js and MySQL)

Billing Service handles **payment processing** using the **Stripe API**.

Step 1: Setting Up Express Server

```javascript
CopyEdit
const express = require('express');
const app = express();
const bodyParser = require('body-parser');
app.use(bodyParser.json());
const stripe = require('stripe')('sk_test_XXXX');

app.post('/pay', async (req, res) => {
    const { amount, token } = req.body;
    const charge = await stripe.charges.create({
        amount,
        currency: 'usd',
```

```
      source: token,
  });
  res.json({ status: "Payment Successful", charge });
});

app.listen(3002, () => console.log('Billing Service running on
port 3002'));
```

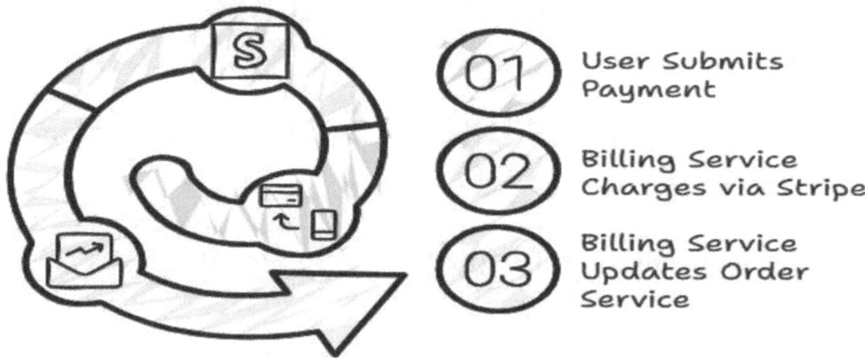

Figure 4-4. Payment Flow in Billing Service (User submits payment, Billing Service charges via Stripe, and updates Order Service.)

Frontend Implementation Using React

The frontend will:

- Display a list of available products.

- Allow users to place orders.

- Show order history and payment details.

Setting Up a React Component

```javascript
javascript
CopyEdit
import React, { useState, useEffect } from 'react';

function OrderList() {
    const [orders, setOrders] = useState([]);

    useEffect(() => {
        fetch('/orders')
            .then(response => response.json())
            .then(data => setOrders(data));
    }, []);

    return (
        <div>
            <h2>Order History</h2>
            <ul>
                {orders.map(order => (
                    <li key={order.id}>{order.product} -
                    {order.status}</li>
                ))}
            </ul>
        </div>
    );
}

export default OrderList;
```

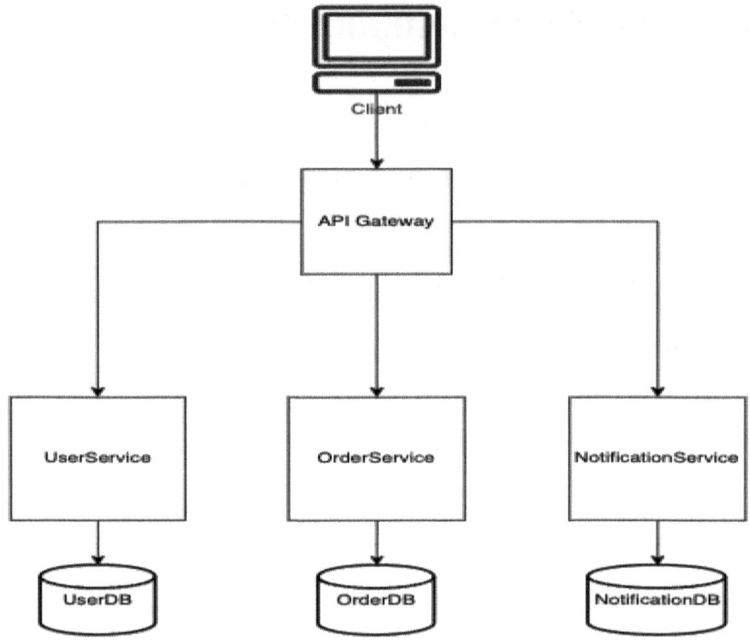

Figure 4-5. ***Frontend UI Interacting with Microservices*** *(Diagram showing React frontend making API calls to Order, Inventory, and Billing Services.)*

Deploying the Microservices Using Docker and Kubernetes

Step 1: Writing Dockerfiles

Order Service Dockerfile

```dockerfile
CopyEdit
FROM openjdk:17
COPY target/order-service.jar /app/order-service.jar
ENTRYPOINT ["java", "-jar", "/app/order-service.jar"]
```

Billing Service Dockerfile

```dockerfile
dockerfile
CopyEdit
FROM node:16
WORKDIR /app
COPY . .
RUN npm install
CMD ["node", "server.js"]
```

docker-compose.yml

```yaml
version: "3.9"

services:
  order-service:
    build: ./order-service
    container_name: order-service
    ports:
      - "8081:8080"
    environment:
      INVENTORY_API_URL: "http://inventory-service:8082"
    depends_on:
      - inventory-service

  inventory-service:
    build: ./inventory-service
    container_name: inventory-service
    ports:
      - "8082:8080"
    environment:
      MONGO_URI: "mongodb://mongo:27017/inventorydb"
    depends_on:
      - mongo
```

```
  billing-service:
    build: ./billing-service
    container_name: billing-service
    ports:
      - "8083:3000"
    environment:
      STRIPE_API_KEY: "test_123456"

  mongo:
    image: mongo:6
    container_name: mongodb
    ports:
      - "27017:27017"
    volumes:
      - mongo_data:/data/db

volumes:
  mongo_data:
```

Step 2: Kubernetes Deployment YAML

```
yaml
CopyEdit
apiVersion: apps/v1
kind: Deployment
metadata:
  name: order-service
spec:
  replicas: 2
  template:
    spec:
      containers:
```

```
    - name: order-container
      image: myrepo/order-service
      ports:
        - containerPort: 8080
```

As microservices grow, managing separate YAML files becomes difficult.

Helm provides:

- Template-based Kubernetes manifests

- Versioning of deployments

- Parameterized values per environment (dev, QA, prod)

- Single-command install/upgrade:

helm install order-chart ./charts/order-service

Helm is the recommended approach for production-grade deployments across multiple microservices.

Example Kubernetes Secret

```
apiVersion: v1
kind: Secret
metadata:
  name: billing-secrets
type: Opaque
data:
  STRIPE_API_KEY: c3RyaXBlX3Rlc3Rfa2V5    # base64 encoded
```

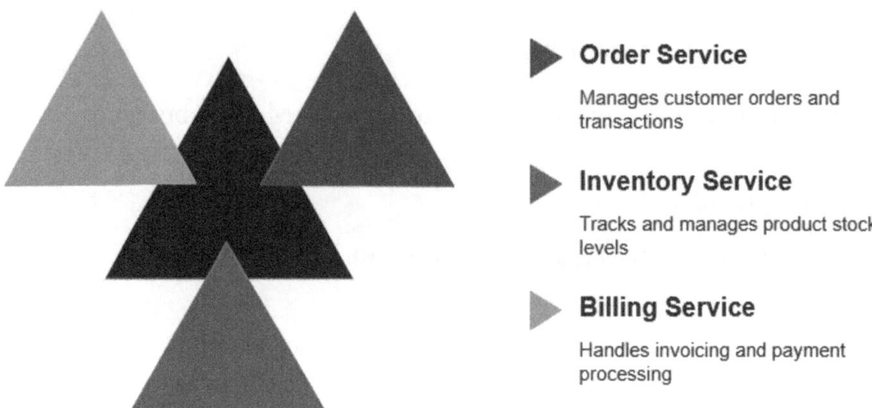

Figure 4-6. Kubernetes Cluster with Order, Inventory, and Billing Services *(Diagram showing microservices running in separate pods within a Kubernetes cluster.)*

Conclusion

The chapter presented the implementation of true microservices architecture to showcase efficient interactions between cloud-based services. We covered:

- The Order and Inventory Services operate under Spring Boot to process orders, manage stock inventory, and provide instant updates.

- A Stripe-integrated Node.js Billing Service is the node that handles secure payment transactions and invoicing operations.

- The frontend component implements a user-friendly interface that consumes APIs to work smoothly with backend microservices.

- The system includes Dockerized microservices that deploy on Kubernetes to manage scalability, create high availability, and maintain fault tolerance through container orchestration.

The deployment of Kubernetes on each microservice through containerization resulted in a flexible system that accommodates business requirements and an increasing user population.

In the following chapter, we will examine monitoring and logging techniques as well as performance improvement strategies to guarantee smooth operation, security, and efficiency in a production environment.

CHAPTER 5

Scaling, Monitoring, and Performance Optimization of Microservices

Introduction

In the last chapter, we already showed the implementation of microservices in a Spring Boot and Node.js with React application and deployment on a Kubernetes infrastructure. Although this architecture forms the basis of implementing microservices, it cannot stand on its own to address the needs of the contemporary business applications. Practical applications should be created in such a way that they are scalable as well as have performance and constant monitoring to ensure maximum functionality of the application under different conditions.

The applications in the modern world have to face various issues: varying workloads, unexpected traffic bursts, and possible system malfunctions. These problems may interfere with user experiences and can bring down performance unless entities are taken to address them.

© Mrinmoy Aich and Diganta Sengupta 2026
M. Aich and D. Sengupta, *Cloud-Native Modernization Unleashed,*
https://doi.org/10.1007/979-8-8688-2379-4_5

In order to satisfy these needs, organizations need to deploy systems capable of scaling dynamically to match load, continuously check the health of their applications, and optimize performance dynamically.

In this chapter, attention will be paid to the ways of meeting these needs by discussing several major issues:

- **Scaling Microservices Dynamically**: We will discuss how Kubernetes and load balancing systems can be applied to dynamically scale microservices vertically and horizontally so that the system can support more demand without having to slow down.

- **Monitoring Tools of Real-time System Performance**: We will present observability tools such as Prometheus and Grafana, which will allow monitoring real-time performance of systems, resource consumption, and health of applications.

- **Prometheus, Grafana, and ELK Stack Monitoring and Logging**: We will explore further the use of Prometheus, Grafana, and ELK stack in monitoring application metrics and logs in real-time so that the potential problems are identified and resolved in a timely manner.

- **Optimization Methods of Performance**: Lastly, we shall discuss different methods of optimizing the performance of microservices, such as caching, database indexing, and asynchronous processing, all of which are meant to decrease bottlenecks and guarantee high throughput.

- After reading this chapter, you will be in a position to design and deploy a modern and scalable microservices architecture that is capable of delivering the best performance and user experience even in the most extreme conditions.

Scaling Microservices with Kubernetes

Why Scaling Is Important?

With a cloud-native environment, the load on applications may fluctuate dramatically as a result of changes in traffic load, season bursts, or a burst in user activity. This flexibility in traffic may cause an enormous load on the performance of a system when scaling is not well controlled. In order to achieve the best performance and also regulate cost, there is a need to have scaling strategies that enable the application to dynamically scale its resources according to the current load.

Scaling also provides that the applications can scale to performance requirements without excessive provisioning that can result in unwarranted operating expenses. Scaling will also enable organizations to be highly available and reliable even at peak periods without having to deal with it manually. In the absence of scaling, an application might run slowly, be unresponsive or even go offline and result in a bad user experience and even loss of business.

Microservices are specially suited to dynamic scaling since they can be divided into a number of independent services that can be independently scaled according to their respective demand. Kubernetes is an effective container orchestration platform, which offers an efficient mechanism to revise microservices in an automatic manner, allowing companies to react to the fluctuating workloads with minimum effort.

There are two main ways of scaling microservices:

Vertical Scaling (Scaling Up):
Vertical scaling is an extension of the resources (CPU, memory, and storage) given to one instance of a microservice. It is possible by devoting additional resources to the already running container, which is functionally equivalent to scaling up the instance to be able to cope with

a greater load. Although vertical scaling is a simple solution, it has its limitations. It cannot grow larger than the size of the individual machine or instance and can ultimately enter the zone of diminishing returns as the hardware resources become used up.

Scaling Out: Horizontal Scaling:

The more popular method for cloud-native microservices is horizontal scaling. It is a process that entails the addition of additional instances (or copies) of a microservice in order to distribute the workload. Every new instance processes part of the incoming traffic, which means that the application can be scaled to meet more demand. Horizontal scaling is more usable in the cloud setting as it helps the application to scale indefinitely as constrained by the resources found in the cloud infrastructure. Kubernetes offers a high level of horizontal scalability, having the ability to scale the number of pods automatically and according to some preset criteria.

With Kubernetes, Horizontal Pod Autoscaling (HPA) is an effective tool that can be used to automatically scale the number of pods within a deployment according to observed metrics: CPU utilization or application-specific metrics. With HPA, Kubernetes can be used to make sure that your application is capable of both scaling out (and in) dynamically in response to changing demand, without human intervention. This automatic scaling feature enhances the efficiency and responsiveness of the system to changes in real-time traffic.

Implementing Kubernetes Horizontal Pod Autoscaler (HPA)

To enable auto-scaling, we define resource requests and limits in our deployment files.

Step 1: Configure Resource Requests in Deployment YAML

```yaml
yaml
CopyEdit
apiVersion: apps/v1
kind: Deployment
metadata:
  name: order-service
spec:
  replicas: 2
  template:
    spec:
      containers:
        - name: order-container
          image: myrepo/order-service
          resources:
            requests:
              cpu: "250m"
              memory: "512Mi"
            limits:
              cpu: "500m"
              memory: "1Gi"
```

Step 2: Deploy the Horizontal Pod Autoscaler

```yaml
yaml
CopyEdit
apiVersion: autoscaling/v2
kind: HorizontalPodAutoscaler
metadata:
  name: order-service-hpa
spec:
  scaleTargetRef:
```

```
    apiVersion: apps/v1
    kind: Deployment
    name: order-service
minReplicas: 2
maxReplicas: 10
metrics:
    - type: Resource
      resource:
        name: cpu
        target:
          type: Utilization
          averageUtilization:
```

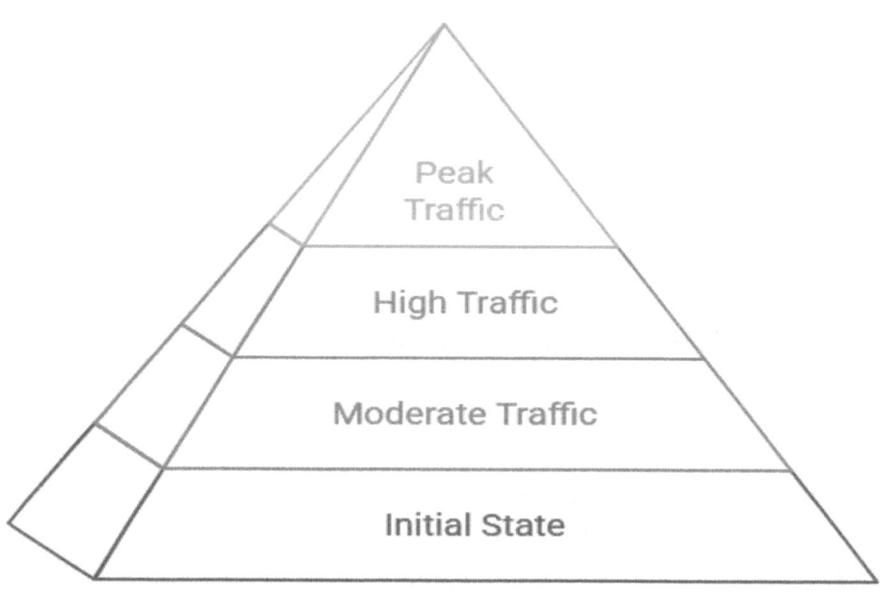

Figure 5-1. Kubernetes HPA Scaling Order Service Based on CPU Usage *(Diagram showing increasing replicas of Order Service when traffic spikes.)*

Monitoring Microservices with Prometheus and Grafana

Why Is Monitoring Crucial?

System integrity depends on reliability and performance excellence, requiring monitoring within microservices-based systems. API-based service communication in distributed systems generates operational failures at three different points: within applications, network connections, and system base elements. Monitoring systems become unstable because inappropriate monitoring methods fail to identify and resolve issues effectively.

The effectiveness of monitoring systems maintains its essential role for three crucial operational elements: efficiency, reliability, and performance quality.

- Real-time system health tracking in monitoring gives users essential system performance data, as well as uptime data and usage statistics about resources. Organizations that continuously check CPU utilization together with memory and network performance data discover and resolve performance blockers before users experience any impact.

- Database monitoring systems detect failures through alerts, enabling prompt response actions to shorten service interruptions. Analyzing failures becomes more efficient since

- The resource assignment process in cloud-native environments relies on currently detected demand requirements. Organizational monitoring offers two-fold benefits: it maximizes CPU, memory, and storage allocation while reducing expenditure costs without affecting operational pace.

- Security monitoring tools provide advanced functionalities to detect unauthorized security breaches and vulnerabilities through their advanced capabilities. Companies achieve compliance standard implementation by tracking their logs and maintaining an audit trail.

- Evaluating metrics allows auto-scaling systems to verify real-time usage changes for automatic resource modifications, ensuring high usage and consistent application performance that benefits everyone.

Running system operations actively through a detailed monitoring program forms the base of modern cloud-native applications. It enables businesses to maintain active system control, decrease downtime, and enhance user satisfaction.

Popular Monitoring Tools:

- **Prometheus**—Collects time-series metrics from microservices.

- **Grafana**—Visualizes Prometheus metrics on dashboards.

Setting Up Prometheus for Microservices

Step 1: Configure Prometheus to Scrape Metrics

Create a `prometheus.yml` file to scrape metrics from our services:

```yaml
CopyEdit
global:
  scrape_interval: 15s
```

```yaml
scrape_configs:
  - job_name: 'order-service'
    static_configs:
      - targets: ['order-service:8080']
```

Step 2: Expose Metrics in Spring Boot

Add the Micrometer Prometheus dependency in `pom.xml`:

```
xml
CopyEdit
<dependency>
    <groupId>io.micrometer</groupId>
    <artifactId>micrometer-registry-prometheus</artifactId>
</dependency>
```

Enable the Prometheus endpoint in `application.yml`:

```
yaml
CopyEdit
management:
  endpoints:
    web:
      exposure:
        include: Prometheus
```

Visualizing Data in Grafana

After Prometheus gathers metrics on different services and infrastructure elements, the raw data can be converted into an action through potent visualization by using Grafana. Grafana is a free open-source tool that is compatible with Prometheus to give real-time dashboards, graphs, and charts. These visualizations can also be used to comprehend application and infrastructure performance and allow teams to rapidly diagnose problems and trends and use data to make decisions.

Lateral and Horizontal Bar Charts: Grafana has the ability to display data in either horizontal or vertical bar charts.

Real-time Dashboards: Grafana enables you to build customizable dashboards that show important metrics, which include response times, CPU usage, memory usage, request rates, and others. These dashboards may be configured to be real time such that they provide a dynamic perspective on the system performance.

Time-series Graphs: Prometheus utilizes time-series metrics as a way to store data, and Grafana is good at presenting those metrics. Time-series graphs are used to demonstrate the movement of metrics over time, which can be used to identify trends, anomalies, and bottlenecks of performance. As an example, you can graphically track CPU usage during hours or days to see spikes of CPU usage and associate those with particular events or traffic patterns.

Alerts and Notifications: Grafana allows one to create an alerting rule with threshold-related metrics. When any metric crosses a defined threshold (e.g., CPU utilization greater than 80% for more than 5 minutes), an alert can be sent in Grafana. The alerts may be delivered to different communication platforms like email, Slack, or PagerDuty, and teams are informed whenever the critical thresholds have been violated.

Request Rate and Latency: In Grafana, it is possible to visualize the response time of services, as well as the request rate (req/s). When these metrics are correlated with each other, you are likely to understand the interaction between traffic and system performance better. As an example, the sudden increase in request rates may cause the rise of latency, which is easy to monitor on a Grafana dashboard.

Multi-source Integration: Grafana is able to integrate with data sources in addition to Prometheus, like Elasticsearch, InfluxDB, or MySQL. This enables the teams to get a complete picture of the application and the infrastructure and combine logs, metrics, and other types of data into a single dashboard.

Example Use Cases:

Service Performance Monitoring: Viewing the response times and error rates by service would help the teams identify which services are performing poorly or having problems. This enables prompt investigation and correction, and hence the performance of the systems is at optimal levels.

System Health Monitoring: Grafana allows visualization of the CPU usage, memory usage, disk I/O, and network traffic, which gives a clear overview of the system health. This information is critical in the detection of resource limitation or hardware failure as early as possible so that it can be remedied before it happens.

Traffic Analysis: Traffic analysis helps teams to monitor the activity of users, which are the busiest days, as well as to allocate resources efficiently. It is particularly useful with scaling microservices dynamically according to the traffic patterns.

Providing organizations with real-time visibility into the health, performance, and resource utilization of their microservices and infrastructure, a feature of the Grafana tool is applied by visualizing the information gathered by Prometheus. Grafana will be a necessary tool to effectively monitor and optimize the performance of microservices-based systems with the possibility to create customizable dashboards, detect anomalies with the help of alerts, and track important metrics over time.

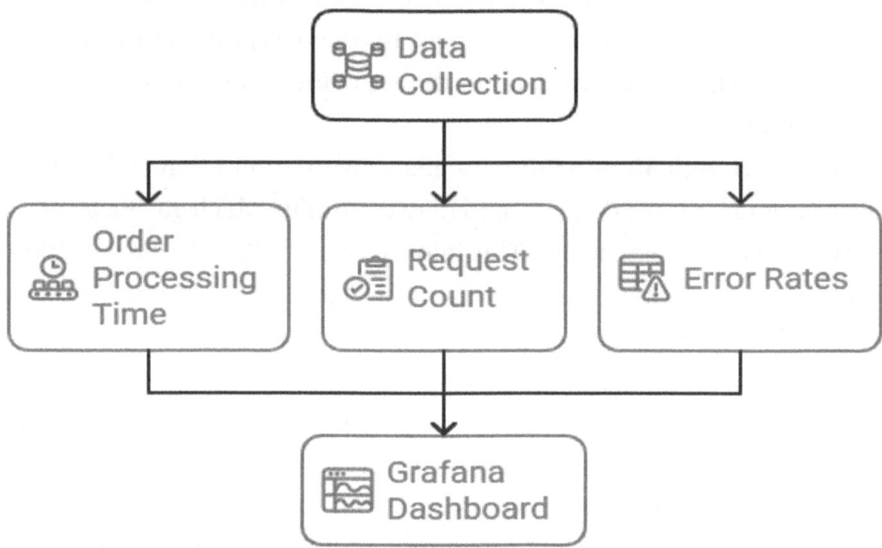

Figure 5-2. Grafana Dashboard Showing API Performance Metrics *(Graph displaying order processing time, request count, and error rates.)*

Implementing Centralized Logging with ELK Stack

Logging Challenges in Microservices:

- Logs are scattered across multiple services.

- Difficult to track user requests across multiple services.

Solution: Use **ELK Stack (Elasticsearch, Logstash, Kibana)** for centralized logging.

Setting Up ELK Stack for Logging

Step 1: Configuring Logstash

Create `logstash.conf` to capture logs from microservices:

```yaml
CopyEdit
input {
  file {
    path => "/var/log/microservices/*.log"
    start_position => "beginning"

output {
  elasticsearch {
    hosts => ["http://elasticsearch:9200"]
```

Step 2: Sending Logs from Microservices to Logstash

Modify the **Spring Boot logging configuration**:

```yaml
CopyEdit
logging:
  file:
    name: /var/log/microservices/order-service.log
```

Now, logs will be centralized and searchable using Kibana.

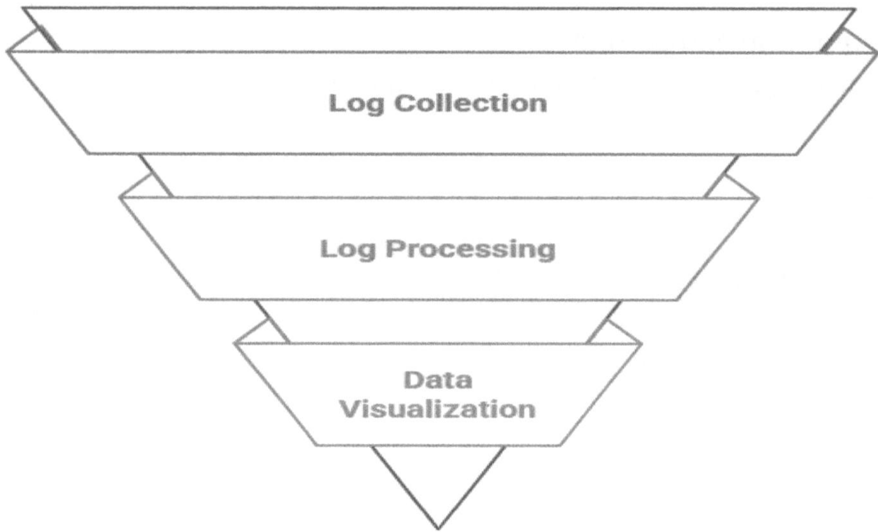

Figure 5-3. ELK Stack Processing and Visualizing Microservices Logs *(Diagram showing logs from multiple services flowing into Elasticsearch and viewed in Kibana.)*

Optimizing Performance in Microservices Caching for Faster API Responses

Caching reduces redundant database queries, improving response time. We use **Redis** as an in-memory cache.

Implementing Redis Cache in Spring Boot

Add Redis dependency in pom.xml:

```
xml
CopyEdit
<dependency>
```

```
    <groupId>org.springframework.boot</groupId>
    <artifactId>spring-boot-starter-data-redis</artifactId>
</dependency>
```

Modify Order Service to cache responses:

```java
CopyEdit
@Service
public class OrderService {

    @Autowired
    private RedisTemplate<String, Order> redisTemplate;

    public Order getOrderById(Long id) {
        return redisTemplate.opsForValue().get("order_" + id);
    }
}
```

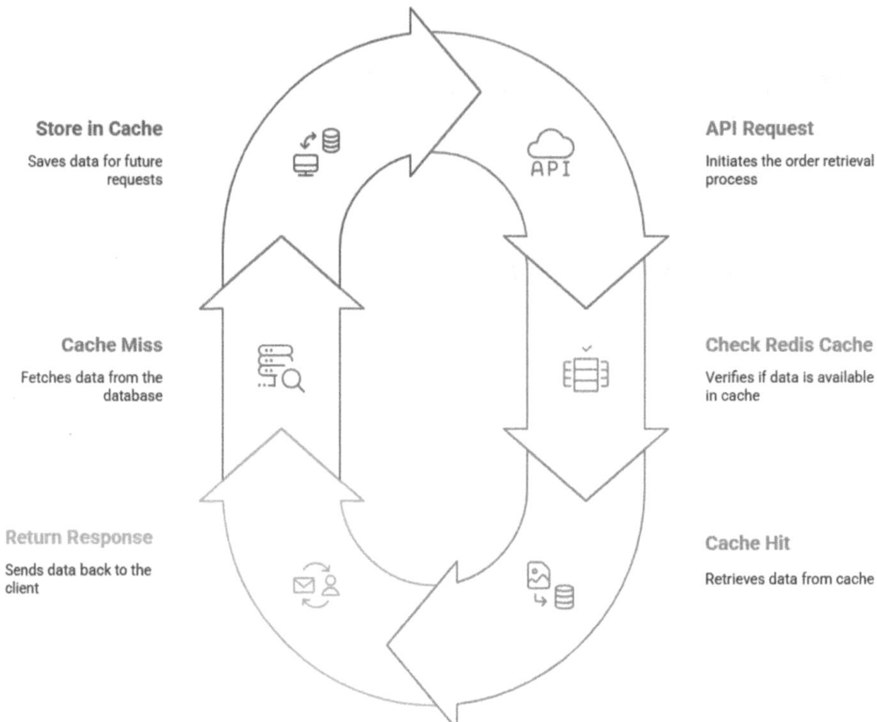

Figure 5-4. Redis Caching Mechanism for Order Service
(Flowchart showing API requests hitting Redis cache before database lookup.)

Optimizing Database Queries

Database queries should be optimized so that microservices can be able to handle large loads of requests without introducing huge amounts of latency. One can easily imagine how inefficient queries may become easily bottlenecks in an application, particularly as the size of the data expands. The methods which may be adopted to enhance the performance are some of the techniques that can be applied in improving the performance, they include indexing, query optimization and efficient joins.

Use Indexing

Indexing is one of the most effective ways of accelerating searches in the database. An index is a structure of information that allows the database to find the rows more quickly, as the index in the book allows you to find a certain page more quickly as well. Without indexes, the database has to scan the entire table, which is highly inefficient, especially when there is much data.

How indexing may be utilized in order to improve a query performance:

Quick Search Processes: Rapid search procedures are also able to save time that is utilized in the searching of the information since they have the fast method of searching.

Better Sorting: Indexes are helpful in the quicker ORDER BY operations, and therefore, the easier it is to sort data successfully.

Efficient Query Filters: The use of indexed columns in the query can reduce the number of rows that will be searched by the database.

Insertion of Indexing in PostgreSQL to Quicken Queries:

The creation of indexes is easy in PostgreSQL. The following is an example of how the index can be created upon a table column:

CREATE INDEX users email on users(email);

This creates a primary key on the email column of the users table. The process of filtered querying in terms of email will be much faster as well because the index will assist the database, as opposed to the entire table.

PostgreSQL Indexes: PostgreSQL contains a number of types of indexes.

B-tree Indexes: It is the default type of index and is good with most variety of queries and it is mostly applied when the queries refer to equality or range (e.g., =, >, <).

GIN (Generalized Inverted Index): It can be used to index the values of the array or whole-text search.

GiST (Generalized Search Tree): It is used with more complicated data, e.g., geometries or spatial data.

Optimize Joins

Joins are needed to combine the data of over one table, but this can be expensive in terms of performance, especially when dealing with the big tables. Join optimization may also play a crucial role in reducing the time taken to execute queries.

Ways to Optimize Joins:

Denormalization: There are cases when it is preferable to have the data denormalized (i.e., to include unnecessary information in the table) in order to avoid the necessity to make joins. This can be improved to make performance better, but it comes at the price of increased storage and consistency.

An example could be that to obtain user-related orders, you can make a join of a users table and an orders table, but you can store the name of the user in the orders table:

```
CREATE TABLE orders (
    order_id SERIAL PRIMARY KEY,
    order_date DATE,
    user_name VARCHAR(255),
    amount DECIMAL
);
```

Even though this technique saves on joins, it also complicates maintenance of data. The orders table would be forced to be updated whenever the name of the user would be altered.

Only the Appropriate Join Types: It may be useful to apply a specific type of join that would be more efficient in the situation of the query. Indicatively, INNER JOIN can be superior to LEFT JOIN where there is no necessity to have the rows in one table that lack the corresponding rows in the other table.

```
SELECT u.name, o.amount
FROM users u
SELECT u.user id, o.reply date, o.text, o.-o.user id, o.o.text,
o.o.reply date, o.o.text, o.o.text, o.o.reply date, o.o.text,
o.o.text, o.o.text, o.o.text, o.o.text, o.o.text, o.o.text,
o.o.text, o.o.text, o.o.text, o.o.text, o.o.text, o
```

This is normally more effective than a LEFT JOIN that fetches all the rows in the left table even when there is no match in the right table.

Join Columns Indexes: It is necessary to ensure that the columns on which the joining is done are indexed. Suppose you have frequently been executing two table joins on the user-id then the user-id columns of the two tables can be indexed to allow the join to be much quicker.

In order to facilitate the work of microservices and process the growing volume of data and traffic, databases need to be optimized and their operation improved. The use of methods such as indexing, optimization of joins, and denormalization can indeed be of great help in improving the query performance. The advantage of indexing is that it results in faster search and retrieval, but the advantage of joins can be made by reducing the number of expensive operations and also indexing the columns involved in the join, which enables the database to scale. Through these optimizations, you can optimize your application in a way that as the volume of data to be handled increases, the application can support high performance.

Adding Indexing in PostgreSQL for Faster Queries

```sql
CopyEdit
CREATE INDEX idx_order_status ON orders(status);
```

Implementing Asynchronous Processing

Using synchronous communication methods within microservices themes results in performance sluggishness arising from service calls to external APIs, database inquiries, and extensive data processing operations. The system uses RabbitMQ as a message broker to achieve asynchronous processing, decreasing slow requests and boosting system efficiency.

Why Use Asynchronous Processing?

- The background processing enables requests to execute directly while the primary operations continue, making the application more responsive and lightning-fast.

- The messaging queue functions as a processor to handle tasks, enabling services to maintain consistent CPU utilization and prevent system failures.

- The service scalability benefit of RabbitMQ occurs because consumers can scale horizontally to process a growing workload volume.

- Messages stored within the queue maintain reliability because they continue waiting for processing until successful completion, even during failure events.

How RabbitMQ Enables Asynchronous Processing?

Message broker RabbitMQ serves as a platform that supports microservice communication across events. The platform allows users to publish messages to queues from one service without interfering with the individual operations of another service, which consumes and processes these messages separately.

1. The producer service, which operates an order service, uses RabbitMQ to transmit messages when new orders emerge.

2. The RabbitMQ queues the message for reliable storage until one of its consumers retrieves it.

3. The payment service retrieves the queued message from the Consumer Service to run processing operations without delaying primary system operations.

The Order Processing System is a practical use case to demonstrate why Bunnies MQ is an excellent messaging system solution.

A user completes their purchase using an e-commerce application that connects through RabbitMQ to the producer service.

- An order confirmation message gets transmitted from the Order Service to RabbitMQ.

- The Payment Service receives the message from RabbitMQ through an asynchronous mechanism to process payments and update system records.

- The Inventory Service receives order messages, which causes it to update stock information.

- The implementation of RabbitMQ for asynchronous processing improves microservices-based system scalability, reliability, and resource utilization while ensuring better user responses.

Step 1: Configure RabbitMQ

```yaml
CopyEdit
spring:
  rabbitmq:
    host: localhost
    port: 5672
```

Step 2: Publish Messages Asynchronously

```java
CopyEdit
@Autowired
private RabbitTemplate rabbitTemplate;

public void placeOrder(Order order) {
    rabbitTemplate.convertAndSend("orderQueue", order);
}
```

Figure 5-5. Asynchronous Order Processing Using RabbitMQ
(Diagram showing orders being queued instead of blocking API requests.)

Conclusion

This chapter evaluates strategies that advance microservice performance whenever users expand their systems while ensuring dependability and performance throughout cloud environments. We discussed:

- Kubernetes HPA enabled our solution to develop a deployment system based on Horizontal Pod Autoscaling HPA service for automated microservice resource scaling, which supported performance at low operating costs.

- The two components, Prometheus and Grafana, work together to deliver performance and resource consumption reports and health status information. The setup enables users to detect system issues in advance, thus enabling increased incident resolution speed.

- The application applies a unified platform of Elasticsearch Logstash and Kibana (ELK Stack) as its central logging system to acquire and process log information from each microservice, enhancing security audits and system debugging functions.

- System performance was enhanced through four important elements that work together: Redis caching, database indexing, and RabbitMQ async processing.

The scalable architecture of our microservices-based application reaches its full potential in terms of robustness, efficiency, and load capacity because scaling methods unite monitoring enhancements with performance improvements.

CHAPTER 6

Securing Microservices— Authentication, Authorization, and API Security

Introduction

As we transition from monolithic applications to microservices, security becomes a key challenge due to the distributed nature of the architecture. Traditional security models no longer suffice, and we must implement robust mechanisms for authentication, authorization, and securing inter-service communication.

© Mrinmoy Aich and Diganta Sengupta 2026
M. Aich and D. Sengupta, *Cloud-Native Modernization Unleashed,*
https://doi.org/10.1007/979-8-8688-2379-4_6

In this chapter, we will cover

- **Authentication Strategies:** Using OAuth2, JWT, and API keys

- **Authorization Techniques:** Role-based access control (RBAC) and attribute-based access control (ABAC)

- **Securing API Communications:** HTTPS, TLS, and mTLS

- **Best Practices for Microservices Security**

Authentication Strategies for Microservices

OAuth2 and OpenID Connect

OAuth2 is a widely used protocol for authenticating users in modern applications. OpenID Connect (OIDC) extends OAuth2 to provide identity verification.

How OAuth2 Works:

1. **User requests access** through a client (e.g., web or mobile app).

2. **Client requests an access token** from the authorization server.

3. **Authorization server validates credentials** and issues a token.

4. **Client uses the token** to request resources from the API.

5. **Resource server verifies the token** and grants access.

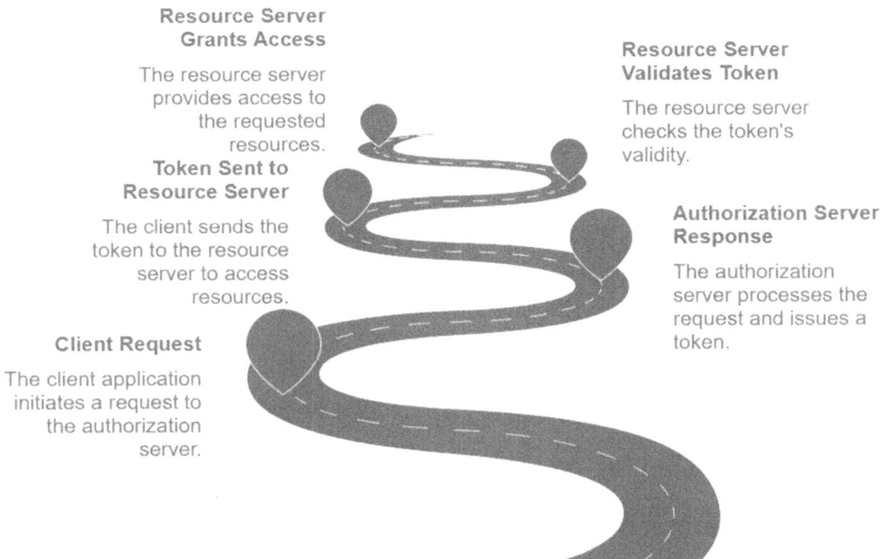

Figure 6-1. OAuth2 Authentication Flow *(Diagram showing token-based authentication flow between client, authorization server, and resource server.)*

Implementing OAuth2 in Spring Boot

Add OAuth2 dependencies in `pom.xml`:

```xml
<dependency>
    <groupId>org.springframework.boot</groupId>
    <artifactId>spring-boot-starter-oauth2-client
    </artifactId>
</dependency>
```

Configure OAuth2 authentication in `application.yml`:

```yaml
spring:
  security:
    oauth2:
      client:
```

```
registration:
   google:
      client-id: your-client-id
      client-secret: your-client-secret
      scope: openid, profile, email
```

JSON Web Token (JWT) Authentication

JWT is a compact, self-contained token for securely transmitting
information between parties. It consists of:

- **Header:** Defines algorithm and token type.

- **Payload:** Contains user claims.

- **Signature:** Ensures integrity and authenticity.

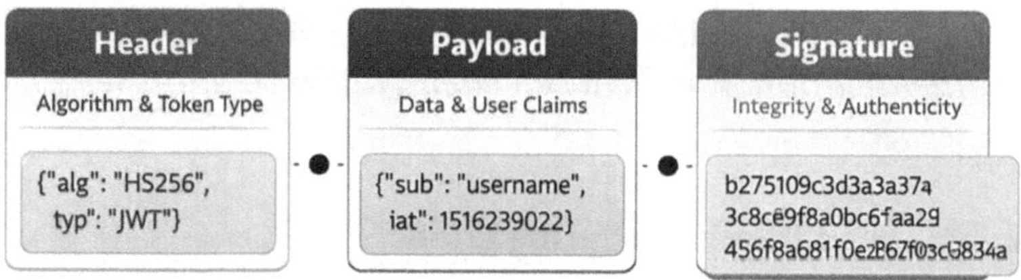

Figure 6-2. *Structure of a JWT Token*

Generating JWT Token in Spring Bootasa
Add JWT dependencies:

```
<dependency>
    <groupId>io.jsonwebtoken</groupId>
    <artifactId>jjwt</artifactId>
    <version>0.11.2</version>
</dependency>
```

Generate and validate JWT in `JwtUtil.java`:

```java
public String generateToken(String username) {
    return Jwts.builder()
            .setSubject(username)
            .setIssuedAt(new Date())
            .setExpiration(new Date(System.currentTimeMillis()
            + 1000 * 60 * 60))
            .signWith(SignatureAlgorithm.HS256, SECRET_KEY)
            .compact();
```

Authorization Techniques

Role-Based Access Control (RBAC)

RBAC restricts access based on user roles. For example:

- **Admin:** Can create, update, delete records.

- **User:** Can only read records.

Implementing RBAC in Spring Boot

Define roles in `SecurityConfig.java`:

```java
protected void configure(HttpSecurity http) throws
Exception {
    http.authorizeRequests()
        .antMatchers("/admin/**").hasRole("ADMIN")
        .antMatchers("/user/**").hasRole("USER")
        .anyRequest().authenticated()
        .and()
        .httpBasic();}
```

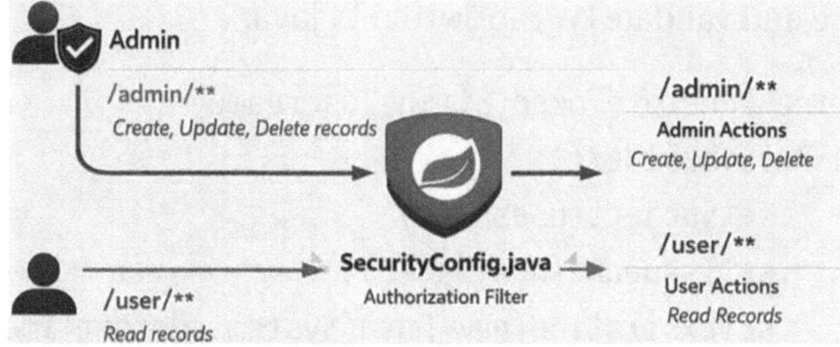

Figure 6-3. *Role-Based Access Flow*

Attribute-Based Access Control (ABAC)

ABAC allows dynamic access control based on attributes such as user
location, device, or request time.

Example of ABAC in Spring Boot

```
if (user.getLocation().equals("US") && user.getRole().
equals("ADMIN")) {
    allowAccess();
} else {
    denyAccess();}
```

Securing API Communication

Enforcing HTTPS and TLS

All microservices communication must be secured using **HTTPS and TLS**.

Enabling HTTPS in Spring Boot

Generate a self-signed certificate:

```
keytool -genkey -alias mycert -keyalg RSA -keystore
keystore.jks -storepass password
```

Configure `application.yml`:

```
server:
  ssl:
    key-store: classpath:keystore.jks
    key-store-password: password
    key-alias: mycert
```

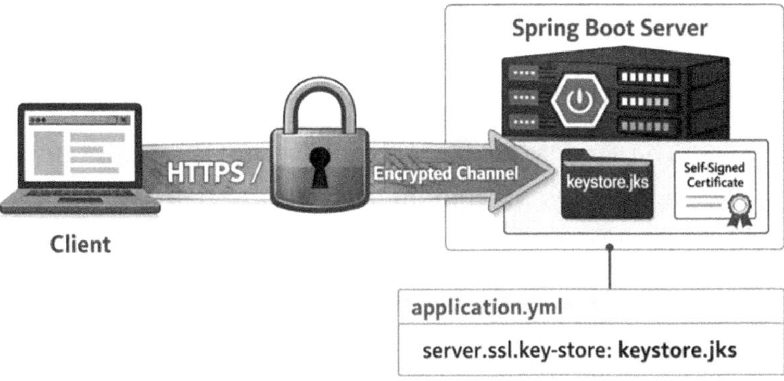

Figure 6-4. Secure API Communication with HTTPS

Mutual TLS (mTLS) for Service-to-Service Security

mTLS ensures both client and server authenticate each other.

The security protocol Mutual TLS (mTLS) improves TLS standards by requiring clients and servers to authenticate each other through mutual requirements. Implementing mTLS provides a vital solution for the secure service communication required in microservices environments.

Key Features of MLS

1. **Bidirectional Authentication:**

   - During mTLS authentication, the parties involved show digital certificates as proof of their identity for mutual verification.

- The authentication process verifies each party as their advertised identity, thus blocking access attempts by unauthorized users.

2. **Encryption:**

   - mTLS's encryption capabilities protect data transmitted between client and server, thus preventing eavesdropping attacks and attempts to tamper with data.

3. **Identity Verification:**

   - The services get their identity verified by certificate authorities who maintain trust.

   - The certification process enables services to build relationships through certificate validation.

4. **Improved Security Posture:**

   - The security solution mTLS ensures authentication between services, preventing unauthorized intrusions and protecting against man-in-the-middle attacks and unauthorized interconnections.

How mTLS Works

1. **Certificate Exchange:**

   - When a TLS handshake occurs, the server demands a certificate from the client.

   - The client delivers its certificate to the server, confirming it against its registered certificate authorities.

2. **Establishing a Secure Connection:**

- A secure, encrypted connection through symmetric encryption gets established after authentication succeeds.

Connection Lifecycle:

- The developed connection remains active from the beginning to the end of the session, offering complete security for all service communication.

Benefits of MLS

- The secure system verifies welfare between only authorized services.

- Data protection through encryption implements a mechanism to secure information that moves during transmission so it remains confidential and maintains its integrity.

- Organizations use mTLS to fulfill their regulatory duties concerning data protection and securing communication channels.

The implementation of mTLS represents a defensive method to protect service-to-service communication in distributed systems, strengthening the security platform of microservices architecture.

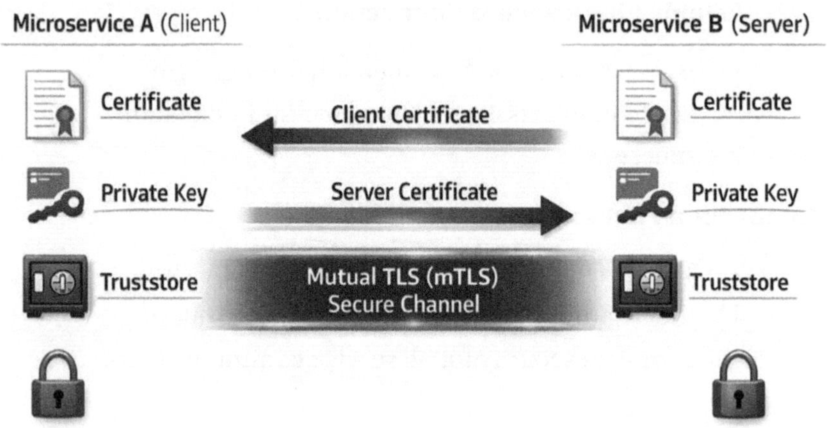

Figure 6-5. *mTLS Authentication Between Microservices*

Best Practices for Microservices Security

- **Use API Gateways** (e.g., Kong, Istio) for centralized security management.

- **Implement Rate Limiting** to prevent API abuse.

- **Store Secrets Securely** using Vault or AWS Secrets Manager.

- **Enable Logging and Auditing** to track security incidents.

Conclusion

This part examined fundamental security systems designed to protect applications based on microservices. We covered:

- The project enhanced authentication security through OAuth2 and JWT authentication protocols to establish easy access control based on tokens.

- The security analysis utilized Role-Based Access Control (RBAC) and Attribute-Based Access Control (ABAC) to realize detailed contextual permission management for users.

- .**Best practices** for microservices security.

- The system achieves API protection by utilizing HTTPS encryption with mutual TLS (mTLS) authentication as its service-to-service authorization mechanism.

The binding of security best practices protects our data against damage. It stops unauthorized access to build strong API security infrastructure that defends microservices from cyber threats while following security requirement.

CHAPTER 7

Continuous Integration and Continuous Deployment (CI/CD) for Modern Applications

Introduction

CI/CD is now an aspect of modern software development to develop reliable, scalable, and rapidly changing applications. Such things as the old-fashioned release cycles, where a software application is not released in weekly or monthly cycles but in fact manually tested and deployed, do not exist in the present new, fast-paced, cloud-driven world. The users desire to be on the same level with the rapid updates, rapid fixes, and

© Mrinmoy Aich and Diganta Sengupta 2026
M. Aich and D. Sengupta, *Cloud-Native Modernization Unleashed,*
https://doi.org/10.1007/979-8-8688-2379-4_7

new features with no interruptions, and companies should be able to deliver them in a sure and constant way. CI/CD may address this need by automating all the stages between the code commitment and deployment processes to allow teams to integrate and test changes to the software and release them with confidence.

CI/CD is all about risk reduction and speed in essence recently. Continuous integration (CI) is a software development model that advances the fact that individuals create their computer code and consistently incorporate the updates into a shared warehouse. Each change entails automatic mechanisms, which encompass compilation, unit testing, and static analysis in such a way that the integration problems can be detected earlier in the release cycle and not at the end of the release cycle. This is further extended with continuous deployment (CD) that enhances the automation of the migration of passing test builds into the staging and production system. This also reduces the level of manual intervention; the likelihood of human error is minimized as well, and the software in code is always as close to the most current stable code as possible.

CI/CD takes place capacitively, especially in microservice design. The development teams do not work on a single large application but on dozens, or even hundreds, of small and deployable services. There are multiple technologies that can be used to build services, which can be serviced by different teams and operate on different infrastructure. Without the properly designed CI/CD pipeline, the structure of the releases, compatibility, and system stability will be a highly complex problem. CI/CD assists microservices to grow on their own and concurrently coordinate perfectly in production by standardization and automation of constructions, inspections, security audits, and deployments.

The cloud platforms have also expanded the importance of CI/CD. The new cloud-native apps are founded on containerization, coordination platforms like Kubernetes, and managed services of cloud providers. The gluing element between the repositories of source code, building tools, container registries, and cloud infrastructure is known as CI/CD pipelines. They allow the teams to package applications into containers, run automated tests and security checks, and push updated images into the cloud in an auditable and repeatable way. This does not only speed up delivery but also enforces uniformity in the development and testing environments as well as in staging and production.

The conceptual and practical aspects of CI/CD will be discussed in this chapter. The bare basics of CI/CD will also be presented, and the reasons why they must be used in systems that revolve around microservices. Next, we are going to consider CI/CD pipeline architecture when applied to modern clouds and show how different components, such as source code control, build tools, test framework, and security scanners, can be combined with one another. The chapter will also involve the step-by-step tutorial of configuring CI/CD pipelines using the popular tools including Jenkins, GitHub actions, and GitLab CI/CD. In addition, we will discuss how it is possible to include automated testing and security checks in the pipeline and how to both deploy microservices to cloud-based infrastructure via containers and Kubernetes. By the end of the chapter, you will have a good understanding of how to design, implement, and optimize CI/CD pipelines that would be utilized in the modern context.

Achieving Continuous Delivery

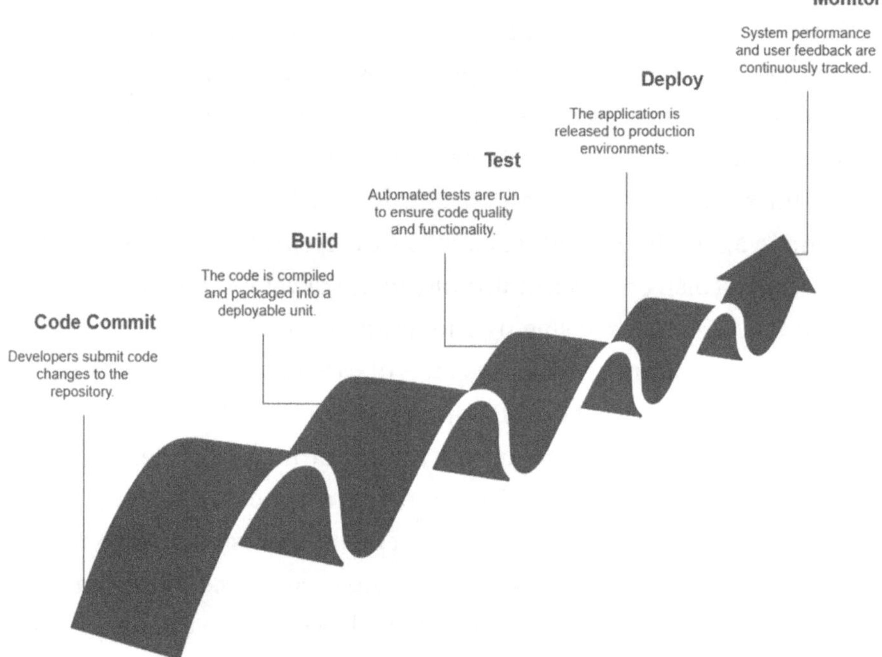

Figure 7-1. CI/CD Workflow (A diagram showing the flow from code commit ➤ build ➤ test ➤ deploy ➤ monitor.)

Benefits of CI/CD:

- Faster release cycles.

- Automated testing and quality assurance.

- Minimized deployment risks.

- Improved collaboration between developers and operations teams.

Understanding CI/CD in Modern Applications

Education Current Practice of CI/CD

CI/CD is among the least complex DevOps practices that are intended to make the software delivery process as fast, unstable, and automatic as possible. Continuous and repeatable processes (CI/CD) are built, deployed, and tested processes rather than infrequent and manual processes that happen when the code changes. It is one of the methods by which teams may recognize the issues at the very first phase, reduce the risks of the integration process, and present the new functions to the users in much shorter periods of time.

Continuous integration is the first pillar of CI/CD. In CI, developers are more likely to push (or, more simply said, merge) their respective code changes to a shared repository, such as GitHub, GitLab, or Bitbucket. The two commits yield to a pipeline that consists typically of unit testing, compilation of codes, code analysis, and packaging. This is to assure that the codebase is such that it can be built and can be tested at any specific time. The problems in integration or the need to make tests failure are easily detected and corrected in the same manner. This would reduce the risks of integration hell, which is steep and uncontrollable in the case of massive and infrequent mergers.

Continuous deployment (CD) is the next step of the CI on the basis of which the code that passed the validation process is deployed directly to the running environment. Upon completing the CI stages (build, test, scan), the pipeline will then be configured to an option of automatically creating deployment of the new version of the application into the staging or production environment. This is also known as continuous delivery within a particular team, and the code is not officially finished; the human being does the last release. The second step is also completely

automated where continuous deployment is in place, which assumes
that all the changes will be carried out in the production process for every
change. This reduces the commitment of discharge lead time and allows
organizations to update in small steps to the degree that is needed more
than once per day.

CI/CD is not just an optimization in the recent deployment,
i.e., microservices and cloud-native, but is also a requirement. The
microservices may be an element of mixed teams, they may be written in
a different language, and they may be deployed separately. This would
entail a large amount of manual coordination and intricate non-CI/CD
coordination. CI/CD also enables every service to have a separate pipeline,
which builds the service, tests it, scans and deploys it, and also integrates
it into the system as a whole. This will enable the growing teams to be
expanded without the performance loss in the stability or quality issues.

Generally, CI/CD transforms the software delivery experience,
a tedious, hand-centric, and error-prone process, into a repeatable,
observable, and automated process. By integrating and deploying on a
regular basis, organizations get an opportunity to respond more quickly to
customer feedback, have less risk to the running of the system, and achieve
some level of the software in the new application environment.

CI/CD Pipeline Architecture
for Microservices

The architecture of microservices is also a complex one, as it presupposes
a great number of autonomous services that should interact and cooperate
to create a consistent application. The services in a microservices-
based system may be created, tested, and deployed individually. This
decentralized quality of microservices requires a dedicated CI/CD pipeline
that will be able to efficiently manage these complexities.

An approach to microservices with CI/CD automates the software delivery process stages, including code commit to deployment, to achieve consistency, reliability, and scalability. The various phases of a CI/CD pipeline specific to microservices are listed below, and their associated tools and technologies are provided.

1. **Source Code Management (SCM)**

   The initial activity of the CI/CD is the source code management (SCM). The source code is managed and version-controlled using tools of SCM such as GitHub, GitLab, or Bitbucket. These are essential tools in the management of the distributed characteristics of microservices, as the microservices could be located in different repositories.

   GitHub: GitHub is a widely used source code management platform with such features as the use of pull requests, code review, and version control.

   GitLab: It has embedded CI/CD functionality and links to repositories to offer continuous integration on the platform.

   Bitbucket: Like GitHub and GitLab, it has other integrations into the Atlassian platform (e.g., Jira, Confluence).

   CI/CD tools are closely coupled with the source code management systems, which causes pictures of automated pipelines to be executed each time code is pushed or merged into a branch.

2. **Automated Build System**

Automating the build process is the next step
that will compile the code and be ready to test.
Such popular build systems are Maven, Gradle,
and Docker.

Maven: This is usually an automation tool for
building that is usually applied in Java. It deals with
dependencies, assemblies, and packaging and
produces an artifact (e.g., a JAR file or a WAR file)
that can be installed.

Example Maven command:

mvn clean install

Gradle: This is an open-source build automation
system that is written to support not only Java
but also other languages and is more flexible and
higher-performing than Maven.

3. **Automated Testing**

In any CI/CD pipeline, including a microservices
architecture, automated testing is an essential part,
as each individual service must be tested before it
is integrated with other services. Auto-tests help
ensure that code modification will not affect the
functionality, and at the same time, they also help in
proving new functionality.

JUnit: This is a popular testing platform of Java
applications. It allows testing of the Java code unit to
be done in order to check that every class or method
is operated as intended.

4. **Security Scanning**

   Since security is paramount to any software
   delivery pipeline, security scanning will identify
   any vulnerabilities in code and dependencies
   prior to deployment. Some of the popular ones are
   SonarQube, Snyk, and Trivy.

   SonarQube: A code analysis tool that is typically
   used to check your codebase in terms of
   vulnerability, code smells, and other possible
   security threats. It is linked with the CI pipeline
   to scan the code automatically after it has been
   committed.

   Example SonarQube command:

   ```
   mvn sonar:sonar -Dsonar.projectKey=my project.
   ```

   Snyk: A tool that concentrates on detecting dependency
   vulnerabilities. It is useful to identify vulnerabilities
   in open-source libraries or containers and can be
   incorporated into the CI pipeline to monitor the new
   vulnerabilities as the code is being built.
   Example Snyk command:

   ```
   snyk test --all-projects
   ```

   Trivy: A container scanner that is used to scan Docker
   images to find vulnerabilities. It is capable of checking
   container images for the known security concerns prior to
   deployment.
   Example Trivy command:

   ```
   trivy image myapp:latest
   ```

Security scanning devices are injected at various stages of the pipeline, and in most cases, before deployment, to make sure the vulnerabilities are identified at an early stage.

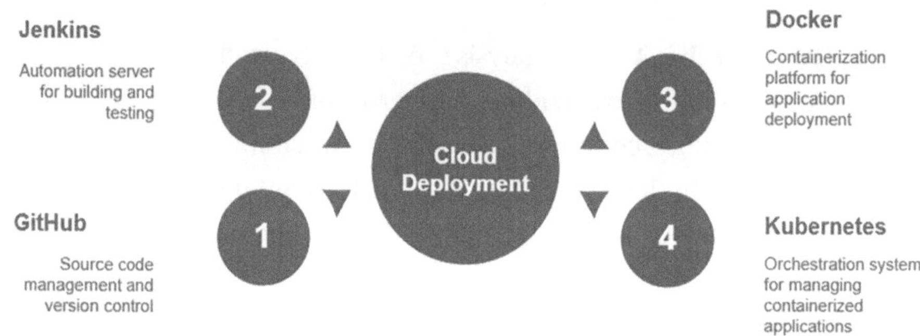

Figure 7-2. ***Microservices CI/CD Pipeline*** *(Diagram showcasing integration of GitHub ➤ Jenkins ➤ Docker ➤ Kubernetes ➤ Cloud Deployment.)*

Setting Up a CI/CD Pipeline

In a CI/CD pipeline, the automation of the code integration, testing, building, and deployment processes is implemented. This facilitates quick and more secure software change delivery. In this section, the process of creating a CI/CD pipeline with the help of such popular tools as Jenkins, GitHub Actions, and GitLab CI/CD will be explained. The main steps of the pipeline, including the integration of the code, automated testing, containerization, and deployment, will be discussed.

Using Jenkins for CI/CD

Step 1: Install Jenkins and Required Plugins

```
sudo apt update && sudo apt install jenkins -y
```

Step 2: Create a Jenkins Pipeline

Go to Jenkins ➤ New Item ➤ Pipeline ➤ Configure.

Example: Jenkinsfile for CI/CD Pipeline

```
pipeline {
    agent any
    stages {
        stage('Build') {
            steps {
                sh 'mvn clean install'
        stage('Test') {
            steps {
                sh 'mvn test'
            }
        }
        stage('Docker Build & Push') {
            steps {
                sh 'docker build -t myapp:latest .'
                sh 'docker push myapp:latest'
            }
        }
        stage('Deploy') {
            steps {
                sh 'kubectl apply -f deployment.yaml'
```

Using GitHub Actions for CI/CD

Create .github/workflows/ci-cd.yml:

```
name: CI/CD Pipeline
on: push
jobs:
```

```
build:
  runs-on: ubuntu-latest
  steps:
    - name: Checkout Code
      uses: actions/checkout@v2
    - name: Build and Test
      run: |
        mvn clean install
        mvn test
    - name: Docker Build and Push
      run: |
        docker build -t myapp:latest .
        docker push myapp:latest
```

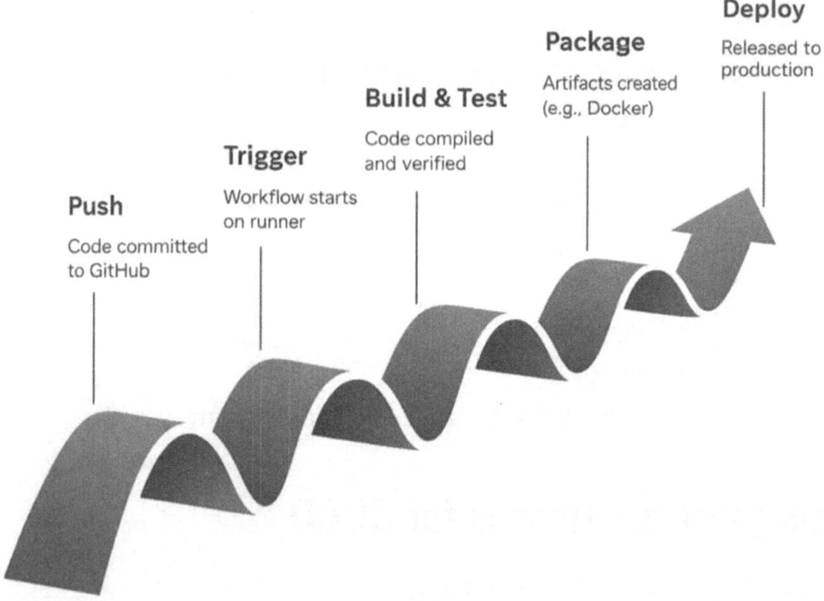

Figure 7-3. *GitHub Actions CI/CD Flow*

Example: GitHub Actions CI/CD Flow

1. **Trigger:**

   - The workflow is triggered by events such as:

   - `push` to the `main` branch

   - `pull_request` creation or update

2. **Job Definitions:**

   - **Build Job:**

     - **Steps:**

       1. Checkout code from the repository.

       2. Set up the programming environment (e.g., Node.js, Python).

       3. Install dependencies (e.g., `npm install`, `pip install`).

       4. Run tests (e.g., `npm test`, `pytest`).

   - **Deploy Job (Runs After Build Job)**:

     - **Steps:**

       1. Checkout code again (if needed).

       2. Build the application (e.g., `npm run build`).

       3. Deploy to a server or cloud service (e.g., using SSH or deploying to AWS).

3. **Notifications:**

   - Send notifications on success or failure (e.g., Slack, email).

Example: YAML Configuration

Here's a simple example of a GitHub Actions workflow in YAML format:

```yaml
name: CI/CD Pipeline
on:
  push:
    branches:
      - main
  pull_request:
    branches:
      - main

jobs:
  build:
    runs-on: ubuntu-latest

    steps:
      - name: Checkout code
        uses: actions/checkout@v2

      - name: Set up Node.js
        uses: actions/setup-node@v2
        with:
          node-version: '14'

      - name: Install dependencies
        run: npm install

      - name: Run tests
        run: npm test

  deploy:
    runs-on: ubuntu-latest
    needs: build
```

```
steps:
  - name: Checkout code
    uses: actions/checkout@v2

  - name: Build application
    run: npm run build

  - name: Deploy to server
    run: |
      ssh user@your-server "cd /path/to/app && git pull &&
      npm start"
```

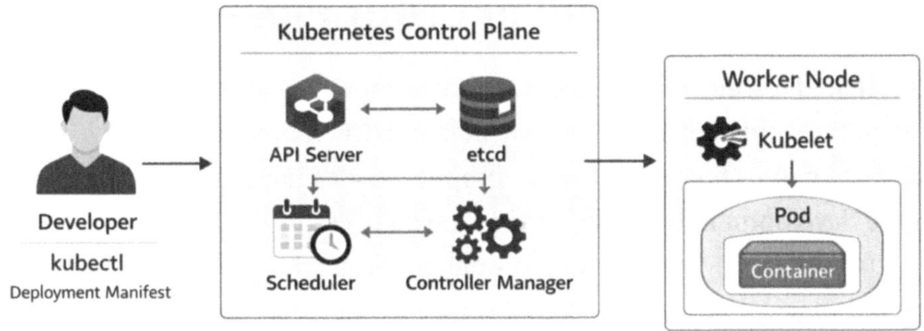

Figure 7-4. *Kubernetes Deployment Flow*

```
apiVersion: apps/v1
kind: Deployment
metadata:
  name: my-app
spec:
  replicas: 3
  selector:
    matchLabels:
      app: my-app
  template:
```

```
metadata:
  labels:
      app: my-app
spec:
  containers:
  - name: my-app-container
    image: my-repo/my-app:latest
    ports:
    - containerPort: 80
```

Automated Testing in CI/CD Pipelines

Automated testing has a very significant component of continuous
integration and continuous deployment (CI/CD) pipelines. The CI/CD
process enables the teams to test computer code changes at every stage
of the development lifecycle, such as the code commit phase and the
production deployment phase, through automated testing. This reduces
the risk of bugs, improves the quality of software, and also optimizes
the delivery cycles. Automated tests could be run every time a code is
introduced in the repository, and it is easier to detect the issue and correct
it at an early stage before it reaches production.

This part will talk about the various types of automated tests that may
be added to a CI/CD pipeline, including unit tests, integration tests, and
end-to-end tests. We shall also take into consideration part of the tools that
are popularized in automated testing in the CI/CD environment.

Unit Testing with JUnit

Unit testing refers to testing of a final unit or a part of the code (e.g., a
function or a method) separately. This will be done to make sure that the
various parts of the program are functioning as per the requirements, and

once this has been done, they will be incorporated with the other parts.
The most prevalent type of tests that are conducted in a CI/CD pipeline is
unit tests, as they are quick and relatively inexpensive to conduct.

JUnit is one of the most famous unit test writing frameworks that may
be used in Java-based applications. It will help to write and test and ensure
that all the code is operational. The tests are automated; therefore, they
can be auto-executed when new code has been pushed into the repository.

Add JUnit dependency in `pom.xml`:

```xml
<dependency>
    <groupId>junit</groupId>
    <artifactId>junit</artifactId>
    <version>4.13.2</version>
    <scope>test</scope>
</dependency>
```

Example Test Case:

```java
@Test
public void testAddition() {
    assertEquals(5, Calculator.add(2, 3));
```

API Testing with Postman and Newman

To Run API Tests in CI/CD:

The API testing is to make sure that the API of the application is
performing as desired, responding to and receiving requests properly.
API tests in a CI/CD pipeline are used to ensure that a microservice is
able to communicate with the other microservices. Postman is also used
widely to develop and test APIs, and Newman is the companion tool on the
command line that enables the use of Postman collections (a collection of
tests) to be automatically executed in CI/CD pipelines.

Example of Postman API Test:

Prepare a set of API tests within Postman (e.g., the tests of GET and POST requests of a user service).

Export the Collection in the Form of a JSON:

Installation Collection: Use the Newman tool to execute the collection in a CI/CD toolchain:

```
newman run mycollection.json -e myenvironment.json
```

Security in CI/CD Pipelines

Since the automation of software development and delivery has become more important in organizations that are dependent on CI/CD pipelines, securing such pipelines is of utmost importance. On the one hand, CI/CD makes software releasing faster and more efficient; on the other hand, it brings new security issues, especially when dealing with code, dependencies, and configurations at all levels of the pipeline. Building a CI/CD pipeline and its subsequent software to ensure its own security is a necessary step to protect applications and the underlying infrastructure from vulnerabilities and threats.

This section suggests the ways to implement security best practices into your CI/CD pipeline, such as static code analysis, container security, secrets management, and vulnerability scanning. We will also analyze the trending tools that are employed to provide security at different pipeline points.

SonarQube with Static Code Analysis

Code analysis that is not executed is called a static code analysis. This is usually done to determine the possible security vulnerabilities, code quality problems, and breaches of best practices. By incorporating the

use of a static code analysis into the CI/CD pipeline, one can make sure
that the vulnerabilities will be found before the code is likely even to be
compiled and deployed.

One of the most popular tools of static code analysis is SonarQube.
It inspects source code with bugs, vulnerabilities, code smells, and
security vulnerabilities and reports in detail these to developers with
recommendations on how to improve them.

How SonarQube Works:

SonarQube is incorporated into the CI/CD pipeline, which is usually
done in the build step.

When a developer commits code, SonarQube will perform a scan
of the source code, searching for security vulnerabilities, including SQL
injections, overflows, and insecure APIs.

It produces a report, which identifies the problems and gives practical
suggestions on how to do away with them.

In case of critical vulnerabilities discovered, the pipeline may be
configured to fail, and the next stage of code is not to be proceeded with.

SonarQube Jenkins Integration:

```
sonar-scanner -Dsonar.projectKey=myproject -Dsonar.host.
url=http://localhost:9000
pipeline {
    agent any
    stages {
        stage('Code Quality Check') {
            steps {
                script {
                    sh 'mvn sonar:sonar -Dsonar.projectKey=
                    my_project -Dsonar.host.url=http://
                    localhost:9000'
```

Container Security Scanning

Use of microservices as containers implies that container images are important to secure. Security exploits are common such that the security application bundles together the dependencies and the application. An attack on the application may occur when it is deployed in production, which is caused by a vulnerability in any aspect of the container, such as the code itself, dependencies, or base image.

Trivy is an open-source vulnerability scanner that has been used to scan Docker images. It checks the application code as well as the dependencies they have to detect vulnerability in the system packages, operating system libraries, and the application code that is known.

Container scanning should be integrated by means of how:

After building the Docker image, the security scan can be performed as a CI pipeline.

Base image vulnerability checks, dependency vulnerability checks, and configuration vulnerability checks.

The vulnerabilities can be identified, and the pipeline can be configured to fail to halt the deployment process until the problems have been resolved.

Scan Docker images with Trivy:

```
trivy image myapp:latest
```

Deploying Microservices to Cloud

Implementation of microservices to the cloud entails a number of strategies and best practices that can make the services scalable, resilient, and simple to manage. Cloud computing platforms, including AWS, Google Cloud, and Azure, offer a great variety of tools and services that can be used to implement the microservices architecture. Here we will discuss the necessary procedures of implementing microservices to the cloud, taking into account the application of Kubernetes and containerization solutions.

Containerization with Docker has been developed in recent years, and it is presently being embraced more broadly.

Docker Containerization

Containerization has gained broader adoption in recent years, and it is currently being embraced by a wider audience.

One technology in the deployment of microservices is containerization. It consists of wrapping up an application and its dependencies in a container, which can be executed in any environment in a consistent manner. Containers are resource efficient and scalable and offer isolation, which makes them best suited to microservices.

Docker is normally used to deploy microservices using containers. Docker allows one to establish, deploy, and manage containers. A microservice is deployed as a Docker image, and this image contains the code of the application, libraries, and configuration files required to execute the service.

Kubernetes Deployment

Kubernetes is an open-source container orchestration system that executes the deployment, expansion, and management of containerized applications in an automatic manner. Implementation of microservices in Kubernetes allows organizations to effectively manage their services with regard to scalability, availability, and resilience. Within this section, we shall discuss the key procedures in the deployment of microservices on a Kubernetes cluster and how Kubernetes manages applications on the cloud.

Example `deployment.yaml`:

```yaml
apiVersion: apps/v1
kind: Deployment
metadata:
  name: myapp
spec:
  replicas: 3
  selector:
    matchLabels:
      app: myapp
  template:
    metadata:
      labels:
        app: myapp
    spec:
      containers:
      - name: myapp
        image: myapp:latest
        ports:
        - containerPort: 8080
```

Apply Kubernetes deployment:

```
kubectl apply -f deployment.yaml
```

Kubernetes Orchestration

Docker is easy to use in containerizing microservices, while Kubernetes is
normally used in the coordination or automatization of the deployment,
scaling, and administration of containerized applications.

Kubernetes can also provide you with an abstraction layer so that you can operate a cluster of microservices that will be a collection of containers and ensure that you can deploy, scale, and maintain those. Kubernetes is an open-source system that can be utilized to manage a cluster of nodes (physical or virtual machines) and schedule containers to run in the nodes based on the availability of resources.

Kubernetes Components:

> **Pods**: This is the smallest unit of Kubernetes, and it can include one or multiple containers. An operating application is described as the period when a single instance of an application is used.

> **Services**: Kubernetes services enable pods to interface with external clients and develop an abstraction of the underlying pods and incorporate a stable endpoint.

> **Deployments**: A deployment will also take charge of creating and scaling pods and ensure the number of replicas necessary is up at a given time.

Kubernetes Cloud Infrastructure Installation

To deploy microservices to the cloud with the aid of Kubernetes, you will need a cloud-based Kubernetes service, either Amazon EKS (Elastic Kubernetes Service), Google Kubernetes Engine, or Azure AKS (Azure Kubernetes Service). Such services provide Kubernetes clusters, which are operated and therefore render the procedure of establishing and supporting Kubernetes on cloud infrastructure to be simple.

Installation steps to install cloud-based Kubernetes:

- **Build a Kubernetes Cluster**: Customers are able to use the Kubernetes service of their cloud provider to build a cluster with the amount of nodes required.

- **Install kubectl**: It is possible to communicate with the cluster using the command-line tool (kubectl). Ensure that you have the right credentials for kubectl to get access to your cloud cluster.

- **Deploy Microservices**: Deployment of your Kubernetes deployment files to the cluster can be deployed with the use of kubectl apply kubectl apply -f deployment.yaml.

- **Scale Services**: Scaling on demand in your microservices by accessing inherent capabilities of Kubernetes to scale either up or down based on the traffic or usage of the resource.

The implementation must be monitored.

Once your microservices are deployed to the cloud, then you can also use continuous deployment (CD) pipelines, which automatically deploy any change to the production environment in case of any change. One can do it with the assistance of CI/CD tools like Jenkins, GitLab CI, or GitHub actions.

In addition to this, microservices within the cloud cannot be managed without surveillance and tracking. Prometheus and Grafana are used to monitor and raise alerts, and the ELK Stack (Elasticsearch, Logstash, and Kibana) is also used to log and analyze application logs.

Microservice Deployment on the Cloud: Best Practices

Isolate with Containers: Microservices are to be enclosed in containers that will offer increased isolation and subsequent scale and management.

Horizontal Pod Autoscaler: Horizontal Pod Autoscaler (HPA) is another Kubernetes mechanism that can be employed to scale the number of replicas automatically based on the CPU/memory utilization.

Use Blue-Green Deployments: Have blue-green deployment methods to ensure the deployment of zero-downtime. Kubernetes can do rolling updates and can be employed to do blue-green deployment via services and deployment plans.

Monitor and Log Continuous: It is done by ensuring that the real-time information about the performance of microservices, their usage, and the errors is continuously monitored and logged.

The deployment of microservices in the cloud requires a course of action that involves the use of containerization, orchestration, and continuous deployment. A cloud computing provider such as EKS, GKE, or AKS combined with Kubernetes is an impressive method to run the microservices on the scale of the large scale. Organizations can give their microservices high availability and resilience and make them capable of serving dynamic workloads in the cloud with the help of best practices, including automated scaling, no-downtime deployments, and robust monitoring and logging solutions.

Best Practices for CI/CD in Microservices

In order to make CI/CD pipelines of microservices effective and scalable, one should adhere to best practices to increase the speed of successful deployments, and their reliability and maintainability. Not only do these practices aid in the mitigation of the risk posed by frequent deployments, but they also make microservices-based architectures run seamlessly as they develop. Some of the most critical best practices to employ CI/CD in the microservices can be listed below:

1. **Apply Environment Consistency in Use Infrastructure as Code (IaC).**

   The concept of Infrastructure as Code (IaC) is all about managing and provisioning infrastructure using code and not only providing consistent, repeatable, scalable, environments. Using IaC, it is possible to specify your infrastructure needs (e.g., virtual machines, networking, and storage) in configuration files, and then version control, automation, and collaboration become simpler.

   Benefits of IaC in CI/CD:

   Environment Replication: IaC provides that all development, staging, and production environments are the same, and environment drift is removed, as well as the problem of it works on my machine.

   Scalability and Flexibility: The scalability of the infrastructure can be easily altered up or down based on the demand, and resources are added or removed automatically.

   Automation: Provisioning and configuration of infrastructure should also be automated so that CI/CD pipelines can be made faster.

   IaC Tools: The most common tools for enforcing IaC in a microservices architecture include Terraform, AWS CloudFormation, Ansible, and even Kubernetes YAML configurations.

2. **Adopt Blue-Green Deployment to Achieve Zero Downtime.**

   Blue-green deployment, in which one environment (the blue environment) and one environment (the green environment) are exactly the same, is a deployment strategy. The new application is deployed to the idle environment, and when it is thoroughly tested, the traffic is changed to that of the green environment with a seamless transition with no downtime.

   The advantages of blue-green deployment are

   Zero Downtime: The environmental transition is fast, and it does not ensure that the users will not have their service disrupted.

   Easy Rollback: In case a problem is encountered in the green environment once the switch is done, it is easy to go back to the blue environment.

   Lower Risk: Before the new version is fully deployed to the green environment, there is reduced risk of production problems since the new version is fully tested.

   Blue-Green Deployment Tools: Kubernetes, AWS Elastic Beanstalk, and Azure App Services are all tools that can be used to support the blue-green deployment strategy.

3. **Controlled Feature Releases by use of Feature Flags.**

   Introduced to provide a way to switch certain features on and off, feature flags (or toggles) enable a developer to switch between different features without requiring new code. This offers the flexibility of incremental release of new features and also contributes to minimizing the risks of deploying untested functionality or unfinished functionality.

Benefits of Feature Flags:

Phased Introduction: There can be features that are switched on to a select group of users to get feedback before rolling out on a large scale.

Continuous Delivery: This is a feature that allows the delivery of code to production continuously, and features remain hidden until it is time to enable them.

Quick Rollback: In case a new feature has trouble, one can disable it on the spot without rollback or redeployment.

Feature Flagging Tools FeatureToggle, Unleash, and LaunchDarkly are the popular feature flagging tools used in a CI/CD pipeline.

4. **Surveillance Pipelines With Grafana and Prometheus.**

   Observing your CI/CD pipeline also means that problems that may arise can be identified in time, and teams can make corrective measures before they impact production systems. Prometheus is a highly functional monitoring system since it captures and records measures, and Grafana offers visualization and real-time dashboards.

**The advantages of the use of Prometheus and
Grafana:**

Live Tracking: Track the performance of the
CI/CD pipeline, e.g., build time, error rates, and
deployment status.

Early Issue Detection: The combination of the
above will help release bottlenecks or failing tests on
the pipeline fast, hence fast responses.

Visual Dashboards: Grafana enables one to create
custom dashboards to visualize pipeline data to
help a team easily interpret and take action on the
visualized information.

Integration: Prometheus can be used to scrape
metrics of CI/CD tools such as Jenkins, GitLabs CI,
or GitHub Actions, whereas the gathered metrics can
be visualized using Grafana as readable dashboards.

5. **Apply Automated Logs in Enforcement and Auditing.**

In the case of microservices architectures, it is
important to stay within the industry standards and
regulations, especially in the case of sensitive data.
Automated logs are detailed accounts of all the
activities undertaken by the pipeline, which makes it
transparent and traceable.

Benefits of Automated Logs:

Audit Trails: Maintain comprehensive records of
the people, dates, and the kind of actions performed
on the pipeline. This is critical in fulfilling
compliance needs, e.g., GDPR, HIPAA, or SOC 2.

Security: Logs may also be used to identify unauthorized activity and misconfigurations or a security breach to the CI/CD pipeline.

Troubleshooting: In case of problems, logs may be priceless in determining the cause of a problem, whether it is during the build process, deployment, or testing process.

Automated Logging Tools ELK Stack (Elasticsearch, Logstash, and Kibana), Fluentd, and Loki (when paired with Grafana) are common options to use when it comes to logging and generating audit trails.

These are some of the best practices that can be followed to make sure that your CI/CD pipelines are reliable, scalable, and efficient. With Infrastructure as Code, blue-green deployment, feature flags, monitoring tools, and automated logging, organizations can not only provide faster code but also more reliable code that is less prone to failure. The practices contribute to the balance between speed in delivery of software and quality assurance, which is highly desired in the current microservices-based and fast-paced settings.

Conclusion

Repeatedly updating software with any type of code became a vital aspect to contemporary programming and, more precisely, to the setting, which depends on microservices and cloud-native software applications. Rather than manual and ad hoc operations of the release cycles, in CI/CD teams can convert code modifications into deployable artifacts in an automatic process pipeline that can be reused. The following chapter has revealed how CI/CD assists in mitigating the friction of the operations and the feedback loop of reducing the reliability of the process of software delivery.

We began with the background knowledge of the fundamentals of continuous integration and continuous delivery. Continuous integration (CI) is oriented toward the combination of code into a common repository on a regular basis, and continuous delivery (CD) is a continuation of continuous integration in which the process of placing proven code into a staging or production environment is automated. CI/CD is obligatory in microservices architectures where dozens, perhaps hundreds, of services are evolving independently to ensure consistency, to prevent service conflicts in integration, or to ensure that frequent changes do not disrupt the system.

The chapter talked of the common CI/CD pipeline architectures using microservices-based applications at the time. An effectively configured pipeline will consist of source code management tools such as GitHub or GitLab, build automation tools such as Maven, Gradle, etc., testing frameworks such as JUnit and Postman, and security scanners such as SonarQube, Snyk, or Trivy. The modern cloud environments are deployed with the backbone of containerization through the use of Docker and orchestration through the use of Kubernetes. Combined, these elements are utilized to offer an end-to-end flow whereby every modification of code is constructed, examined, scanned, packaged, and put into effect with minimal or no manual intervention.

We also touched upon the parts of the implementation of CI/CD in the practical sense with the help of such tools as Jenkins and GitHub actions. Jenkins pipelines enable teams the capability to direct complicated creation and distribute workflows as code, and GitHub actions enable teams to offer a high level of integration with GitHub repositories to automate the build, test, and deploy process for occasions like pushes and pull asks. These illustrations provided us a demonstration of the way we can bring together builds of an application, make Docker images, make Kubernetes deployments, and even build a simple notification mechanism to build a pipeline.

In ensuring that CI/CD pipelines are not just about conducting code fast, automated testing and security checks emerged as a large theme in ensuring the quality and protection of vulnerabilities. Unit tests, API tests, and integration tests that are also run as a part of the pipeline are used to identify the defects during their initial stages of the development life cycle. Before reaching the production stage, the security issues and code smells can be identified with the assistance of the SonarQube code analysis tool and tools like Trivy that allow scanning container images. This left method of testing and security renders the CI/CD pipeline a quality gate that is continuously on as compared to a deployment script.

Lastly, we have examined how microservices can be deployed to the cloud platform using Kubernetes and the best practices that can be used to cement the CI/CD pipeline as robust and scalable. It is Infrastructure as Code (IAC) that offers reproducibility and consistency of environments in their development, staging, and production. The process of deploying the techniques, such as blue-green deployments and feature flags, can assist you and make safer releases and graceful rollbacks. Monitoring and logging continuous monitoring, pipelines, Prometheus as well as Grafana to track the performance of pipelines, the health of the applications and the results of the deployments automated logging and auditing of compliance requirements and traceability across the releases of organizations.

Overall, the current application of CI/CD is not merely a technical pipeline but rather a discipline that is focused on the integration of automation, tooling, testing, and security and observability to provide the fastest and most consistent software delivery. In microservices and cloud-native systems, CI/CD is a requirement to scale development teams, high availabilities, and fast responsiveness to the shifting business needs. Subsequent chapters can build these foundations of CI/CD further with more complex release schemes, incremental delivery schemes, and even more sophisticated incorporation with observability and administration designs, which allow organizations to maximize the advantages of DevOps and modern application infrastructure.

CHAPTER 8

Monitoring Microservices with Prometheus and Grafana

Introduction

Observability is crucial for modern cloud-native applications to ensure reliability, performance, and quick issue resolution. This chapter will cover:

- **Understanding observability in microservices**

- **Logging strategies and tools**

- **Distributed tracing for microservices**

- **Monitoring applications with Prometheus and Grafana**

- **Best practices for effective observability**

M. Aich and D. Sengupta, *Cloud-Native Modernization Unleashed*,
https://doi.org/10.1007/979-8-8688-2379-4_8

Understanding Observability in Microservices

Observability is the ability to measure the internal state of a system based on the data it generates. It consists of three key pillars:

- **Logging:** Capturing application events.

- **Metrics:** Numerical data representing system performance.

- **Tracing:** Tracking request flows across services.

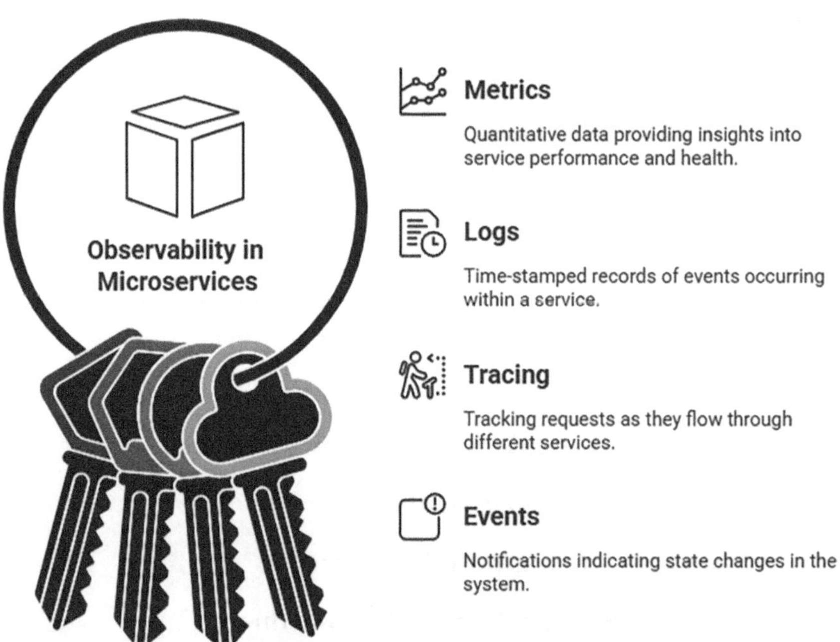

Figure 8-1. *Observability Pillars in a Microservices Architecture*

Benefits of Observability

Modern applications realize various enhanced advantages when developers implement observability features beyond their ability to monitor system health. The real-time system behavior analysis through observability gives operational and development teams quick access to identify and fix performance bottlenecks and operational failures and handle irregular user activities. These following advantages serve as the major benefits of observability:

- **Faster Debugging and Issue Resolution**

  The top advantage of observability helps organizations track down and fix problems at a much faster pace. Teams can follow problems through their multi-service properties by using a data collection system which includes logging and metric recording and distributed tracing. The system interactions become transparent to teams who avoid using blind guesses because they obtain complete visibility throughout the entire process. A delay in checkout processes can be correctly localized by Jaeger or OpenTelemetry to the payment API or order service or database layer through their observability features. Observed systems allow organizations to reduce Mean Time to Recovery (MTTR) to much lower levels.

- **Improved System Reliability and Performance**

  Premarket teams gain the ability to detect emerging system health problems before such issues become full-scale outages thanks to observability. Real-time performance monitoring happens through three key metrics which measure CPU usage as well as memory consumption along with response times. Systems which incorporate Prometheus and Grafana functions provide operators with automatic notification about threshold violations so that they can take preventive steps. The collected observability data helps organizations over time to maximize infrastructure efficiency while improving deployment techniques, which ensures high availability for improved, stable application performance.

- **Better Insight into User Experience and Application Behavior**

  Through observability, users can view interaction data of their applications directly from infrastructure monitoring. Tools that track frontend behavior and user engagement through RUM allow developers to monitor user paths as well as front-end events and client-side error reports. The data provides vital knowledge that both product development teams need to improve application usability and business teams require to measure application effectiveness. The team gains the power to examine and enhance a particular workflow through observability data that shows users are exiting during payment processing.

Logging Strategies and Tools

Logging is essential for debugging and monitoring application health.

Centralized Logging

Microservices generate logs that should be aggregated using tools like:

- **ELK Stack (Elasticsearch, Logstash, Kibana)**

- **Fluentd + Elasticsearch + Kibana (EFK Stack)**

User will choose ELK Stack if they are:

You are already heavily invested in the Java
ecosystem.

You need powerful, complex data transformation
and enrichment capabilities right at the
ingestion point.

You find a specific, indispensable plugin that is only
available for Logstash.

Otherwise, users will use EFK stack when they are:

Performance and a small memory footprint are
critical. This is a major reason many choose Fluentd.

You are operating in a containerized, cloud-native
environment like Kubernetes, where Fluentd is the
de facto standard and a CNCF graduated project.

You require a flexible and efficient way to route
logs from many different sources to multiple
destinations.

Example: JSON-Structured Log Entry

```
{
  "timestamp": "2025-02-28T12:00:00Z",
  "level": "INFO",
  "service": "order-service",
  "message": "Order placed successfully",
  "orderId": "12345"
}
```

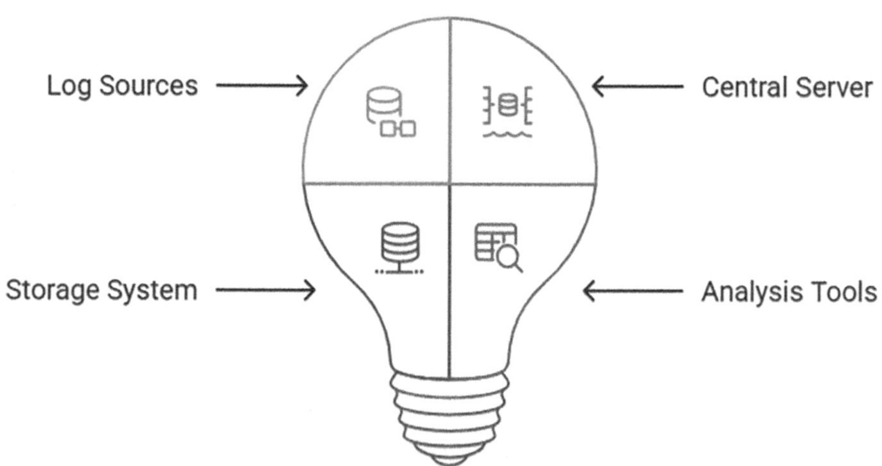

Figure 8-2. *Centralized Logging Architecture*

Implementing Logging in Spring Boot

Use **SLF4J & Logback**:

```
import org.slf4j.Logger;
import org.slf4j.LoggerFactory;
```

```
public class OrderService {
    private static final Logger logger = LoggerFactory.
    getLogger(OrderService.class);

    public void placeOrder(Order order) {
        logger.info("Placing order: {}", order.getId());
```

Distributed Tracing in Microservices

Tracing helps track requests as they travel across multiple services.

Tools for Distributed Tracing

- **Jaeger** (OpenTelemetry-based)
- **Zipkin**

Implementing Tracing in Spring Boot with OpenTelemetry

Add dependencies:

```
<dependency>
    <groupId>io.opentelemetry</groupId>
    <artifactId>opentelemetry-exporter-otlp</artifactId>
    <version>1.15.0</version>
</dependency>
```

Configure tracing:

```
@Bean
public OpenTelemetry openTelemetry() {
    return OpenTelemetrySdk.builder()
            .setTracerProvider(SdkTracerProvider.builder().build())
            .build();
```

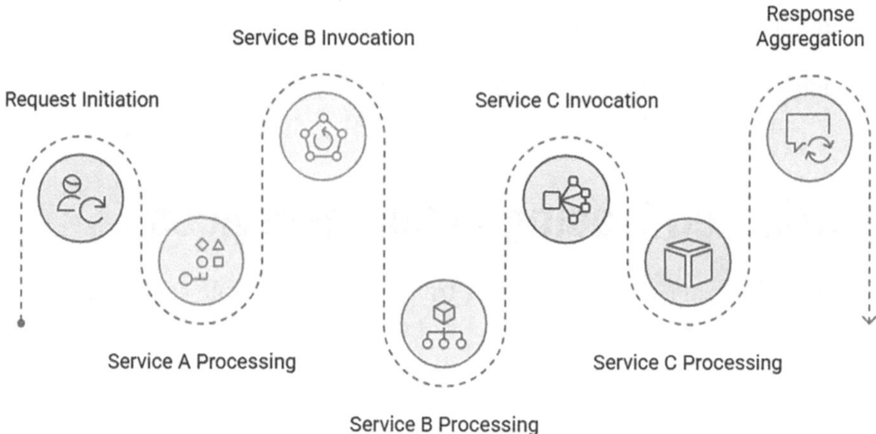

Figure 8-3. *Request Tracing Flow in Microservices*

Monitoring Applications with Prometheus and Grafana

Monitoring provides real-time insights into system health.

For example, in a Spring Boot application, metrics are exposed through Micrometer, which acts as the instrumentation bridge between the application and monitoring backends. When the Micrometer and Spring Boot Actuator dependencies are included, the application automatically publishes a wide range of runtime metrics such as JVM memory usage, CPU load, thread counts, HTTP request statistics, and datasource connection activity. These metrics are made available through the Spring Boot Actuator/actuator/metrics endpoint, and when the Prometheus registry is added, Micrometer formats the data using Prometheus' exposition format at /actuator/prometheus. Developers can also define custom metrics by injecting the MeterRegistry and registering counters, gauges, or timers to capture domain-specific behavior within the service. This setup ensures that the application exposes a consistent set of operational and performance indicators that can be scraped and stored by Prometheus for analysis and alerting.

Setting Up Prometheus for Metrics Collection

Step 1: Install Prometheus

```
sudo apt update && sudo apt install prometheus -y
```

Step 2: Configure `prometheus.yml`

```
scrape_configs:
  - job_name: 'microservices'
    static_configs:
      - targets: ['localhost:8080']
```

Setting Up Grafana for Visualization

Step 1: Install Grafana

```
sudo apt-get install -y adduser libfontconfig1
wget https://dl.grafana.com/oss/release/grafana_8.0.0_amd64.deb
sudo dpkg -i grafana_8.0.0_amd64.deb
```

Step 2: Configure the Grafana dashboard to visualize Prometheus metrics.

Best Practices for Observability

A set of practices with specified consistency and scalability defines the execution of observability. At least four essential best practices exist to preserve visibility alongside performance and resilience within microservice architecture systems.

- Use Structured Logging for Better Searchability

  Microservices should use JSON formats instead of traditional plain text logging. When implemented properly structured logs allow better parsing, filtering and searching within central log systems such as ELK Stack and Loki. The addition of timestamps with service names along with request IDs and user identifiers to logs improves their usefulness during debugging runs and provides better analytics results.

- Every microservice should use a single log format system.

  Log entries created differently by each service within a distributed system result in operational inefficiencies and work chaos. Uniform logging standards need enforcement for all services in the organization. The standardized format allows easy aggregation while making it possible to correlate events as well as investigate the relationships between services.

- Alerts Get Established Through Prometheus Alertmanager

  Application metrics enable developers to build new alerting rules through Prometheus Alertmanager. Users need to establish alert triggers that activate particular thresholds related to application memory resources or system error frequencies and response time abnormalities. Business teams can initiate swift responses to performance failures when receiving alerts, which leads to reduced downtime and smaller effects on operations.

- The system should maintain traceable data between all distributed applications.

  A distributed tracing solution based on Jaeger or Zipkin should be used to monitor requests through multiple microservices. The propagation of trace headers should be a requirement for all services to achieve end-to-end transaction visibility. The practice plays a critical role in finding latency problems while helping to locate bottleneck services and track inter-service relationships.

- Monitor Key Performance Indicators (KPIs) for Better Decision-Making

  Create a system for tracking essential KPI metrics, which include CPU/memory values along with request latency metrics, error rates, service availability metrics, and throughput metrics. Strategic decisions become possible in real time using the Grafana dashboard for visual representation of the measured data. Teams gain the ability to link business objectives with operational performance through KPI monitoring.

By implementing observability best practices, organizations achieve transparent systems and fault tolerance ability as well as operational efficiency and develop a reliable and scalable software environment.

Common Pitfalls: Monitoring a distributed system with Prometheus and Grafana can lead to several recurring issues if the setup is not planned carefully. A common challenge is the lack of consistent naming conventions for metrics across different services, which makes it difficult to compare behavior or build shared dashboards. Another problem arises from the use of labels that produce too many distinct values; this increases the amount of data Prometheus must store and can slow down queries. Teams sometimes expose metric endpoints without proper network controls, unintentionally allowing internal performance data to be accessed publicly. In larger environments, Prometheus servers may also be configured with scrape intervals or retention settings that do not match the actual traffic patterns, causing gaps in dashboards or frequent restarts due to storage pressure. Paying attention to these areas early in the design helps keep the monitoring pipeline stable and easier to operate as the system grows.

Conclusion

In this chapter the author stressed about how important observability remains for maintaining and operating microservices at production level. The ability to observe helps developers and DevOps teams monitor application outcomes alongside performance breakdowns and system failures before end-user encounters affect them.

- Observability in microservices offers more value than single-monitoring practices because it uses combined data from logs, metrics, and traces to show complete system health statuses. Identifying performance bottlenecks together with service interaction examination and reliability assessment depends on this system.

- We examined proper methods for logging alongside approaches to maintain a unified log management system. Through the aggregation of logs from all services under the ELK Stack platform (Elasticsearch, Logstash, Kibana) organizations simplify their debugging operations with better incident analysis and enhanced security auditing.

- Our team employed Jaeger to provide distributed tracing capabilities through the implementation of distributed tracing for better debugging. Distributed tracing helps users detect both problems and latency issues along with service dependencies in complex multi-tiered systems.

- The combination of Prometheus with Grafana enables real-time monitoring, through which we collected metrics with Prometheus while viewing data through Grafana. This implementation framework provides automatic alerts together with computerized responses to problems.

Teams that utilize these multiple observability approaches build robust microservices which deliver better stability alongside reliability and manageability to both users and maintainers for expedited problem resolutions.

CHAPTER 9

AI and Machine Learning in Modern Applications

Introduction

Artificial intelligence (AI) is playing an increasingly crucial role in modern application modernization by enhancing automation, decision-making, and user experience. Integrating AI into applications can help optimize workflows, improve efficiency, and provide data-driven insights. In this chapter, we will explore:

- The role of AI in modern application modernization

- AI-based automation in cloud-native applications

- Practical use cases of AI in microservices architecture

- Implementing AI-driven features in a modernized system

- Security and scalability considerations for AI integration

© Mrinmoy Aich and Diganta Sengupta 2026
M. Aich and D. Sengupta, *Cloud-Native Modernization Unleashed,*
https://doi.org/10.1007/979-8-8688-2379-4_9

The Role of AI in Modern Application Modernization

AI is transforming modern application development by enabling intelligent automation, predictive analytics, and self-healing mechanisms. Some key areas where AI is impacting modernization include:

Examples Use Cases:

Automated Data Cleansing During Migration

Legacy systems often hold decades of inconsistent data. AI-powered cleansing tools can automatically spot duplicate customer records, outdated supplier information, or conflicting billing entries and correct them during the migration process.

- **Intelligent Process Automation**: Automating manual processes using AI-powered decision-making.

- **Enhanced User Experience**: AI-driven chatbots and recommendation systems.

- **Predictive Analytics**: Data-driven decision-making for optimized business operations.

- **Security and Fraud Detection**: AI-driven anomaly detection and threat prevention.

AI Integration in Application Modernization

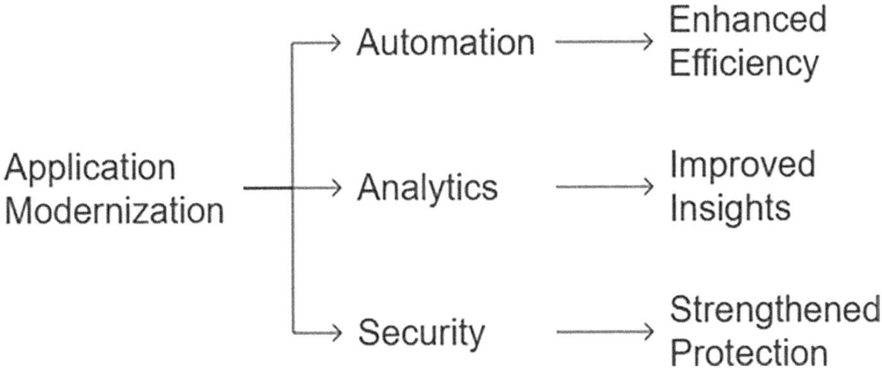

Figure 9-1. AI in Application Modernization (Diagram depicting AI integration in various modernization aspects such as automation, analytics, and security.)

AI-Based Automation in Cloud-Native Applications

Cloud-native applications benefit from AI integration through various automation techniques.

Examples Use Cases:

Intelligent CI/CD Optimization

AI can detect which modules of a large application changed and trigger builds only for those components, reducing pipeline time. For example, in a banking application with dozens of microservices, AI can skip compiling unrelated modules.

AI-Powered DevOps Automation

AI can optimize CI/CD pipelines by automating:

- Code reviews using AI-based code analysis tools.

- Automated bug detection and fixes.

- Smart rollback mechanisms in deployments.

Example: Using AI to detect anomalies in a CI/CD pipeline with tools like Dynatrace AI.

```
name: AI-powered Anomaly Detection
on: push
jobs:
  anomaly-detection:
    runs-on: ubuntu-latest
    steps:
      - name: Run AI anomaly detection
        run: |
          python detect_anomalies.py
```

AI-Driven Cloud Resource Optimization

- **Predictive Scaling**: AI models forecast traffic spikes and optimize cloud resource allocation.

- **Cost Optimization**: AI suggests cost-effective resource allocation based on usage patterns.

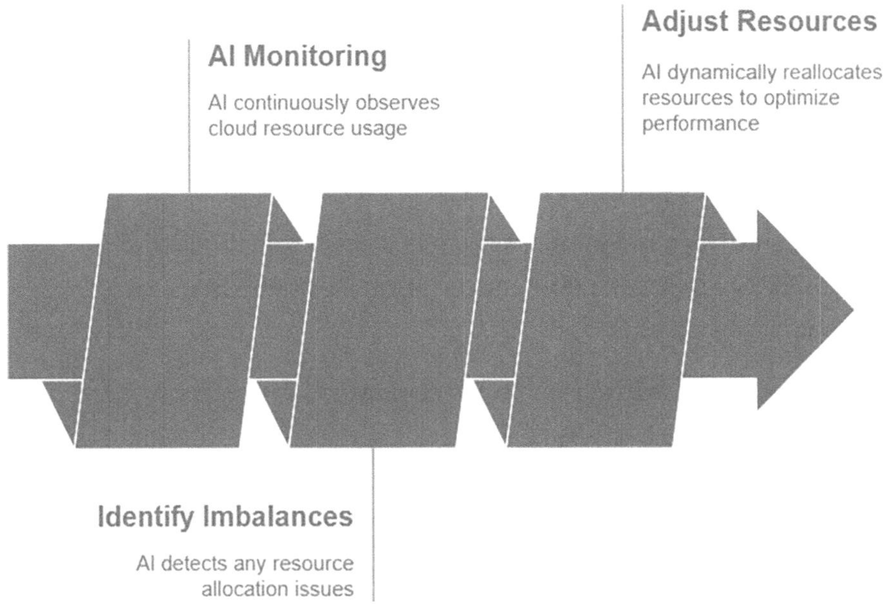

Figure 9-2. AI in Cloud Resource Management (Diagram showing AI monitoring and adjusting cloud resources dynamically.)

Practical Use Cases of AI in Microservices Architecture

AI-Based Chatbots for Customer Service

Microservices-based applications can integrate AI-driven chatbots for better customer interaction.

Example: AI chatbot integration using Dialogflow with a Spring Boot application.

```
@RestController
@RequestMapping("/chat")
```

```
public class ChatbotController {
    @PostMapping("/message")
    public String getResponse(@RequestBody String message) {
        return aiChatbotService.getResponse(message);
```

AI-Enabled Predictive Maintenance

AI can analyze logs and predict system failures before they occur.

Example: Predictive maintenance using AI models in a microservices system.

```
from sklearn.ensemble import RandomForestClassifier
model = RandomForestClassifier()
model.fit(training_data, labels)
predictions = model.predict(test_data)
```

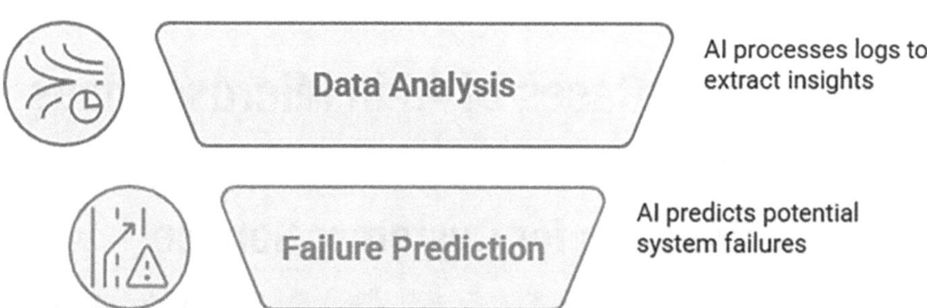

Figure 9-3. Predictive Maintenance in Microservices (Diagram showing AI analyzing logs and predicting failures in real-time.)

Implementing AI-Driven Features in a Modernized System

AI-Powered Recommendation Systems

Modern applications can leverage AI to provide personalized recommendations.

Example: Implementing a recommendation system using TensorFlow.

```
import tensorflow as tf
model = tf.keras.models.Sequential([
    tf.keras.layers.Dense(128, activation='relu'),
    tf.keras.layers.Dense(10, activation='softmax')
])
```

AI-Driven Log Analysis and Anomaly Detection

Using AI to analyze application logs and detect anomalies.

Example: Implementing log anomaly detection using machine learning.

```
import pandas as pd
from sklearn.ensemble import IsolationForest

data = pd.read_csv('logs.csv')
model = IsolationForest()
model.fit(data)
anomalies = model.predict(data)
```

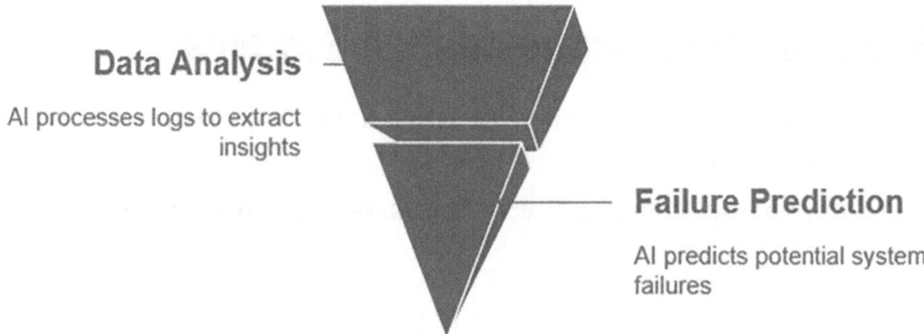

Figure 9-4. AI-Driven Log Analysis (Diagram depicting AI analyzing logs and flagging anomalies.)

Security and Scalability Considerations for AI Integration

Security Challenges in AI-Driven Applications

Example Use Case:

AI Workload Isolation in Multi-tenant Systems

A SaaS application serving multiple clients can isolate each customer's AI model or inference workflow to prevent data leakage across tenants.

- **Data Privacy**: AI models rely on large datasets, raising privacy concerns.

  AI training pipelines typically rely on large volumes of customer data, which naturally raises privacy and regulatory concerns. For systems operating in the EU or dealing with EU citizens, GDPR compliance is mandatory.

For instance, a modernized CRM that uses AI to predict customer churn must ensure that personal identifiers—names, addresses, and purchase history—are either anonymized or processed under explicit consent. The training pipeline may include automated data-masking steps, ensuring the model never stores or reconstructs sensitive fields such as email addresses or account IDs.

- **Adversarial Attacks**: AI models can be tricked with manipulated inputs.

AI systems can be intentionally manipulated by feeding altered inputs designed to mislead the model. For example, a fraud-detection API might incorrectly approve a suspicious transaction if the attacker modifies certain parameters in a way that resembles legitimate patterns. In computer vision systems, the classic case is adversarial images—minor pixel changes that appear normal to humans but cause the model to misclassify. If your application processes uploaded ID documents or meter images, an attacker could introduce subtle modifications that trick the model into accepting a forged meter reading or a manipulated identity document.

Addressing this requires adversarial-robustness testing and model-hardening techniques.

- **Model Explainability**: Ensuring AI decisions are transparent and interpretable.

As AI becomes part of critical decision-making workflows—loan approvals, energy-usage predictions, service-ticket prioritization—systems must provide transparent and interpretable reasoning. Techniques such as SHAP and LIME help developers and end-users understand why a model made a particular prediction.

For example, in a customer-billing dispute module, an explainability layer might show which consumption spikes or meter anomalies influenced the model's decision.

Solution: Implement AI security best practices, including encryption, authentication, and monitoring.

Scaling AI Applications in Cloud Environments

- **Distributed AI Processing**: Using cloud services like AWS SageMaker or Azure Machine Learning.

- **Edge AI**: Processing AI workloads closer to the source for reduced latency.

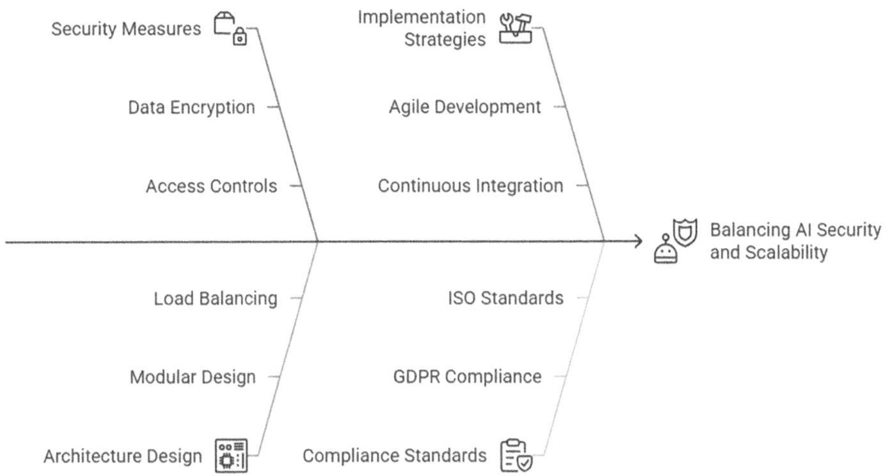

*Figure 9-5. **AI Security and Scalability Considerations** (Diagram showing AI security measures and scalable AI architecture.)*

Conclusion

The chapter investigated how artificial intelligence (AI) strongly affects modern application modernization approaches. Modern technology development implements AI as an operational tool to enhance development strategies and to enhance both application delivery systems and protection measures and sustainment tasks.

The discussion began by analyzing how AI enables modern application redesign through better management systems and automation combined with large-data processing capabilities. The ICommand system installed in contemporary applications enables them to change automatically while reaching intelligent capabilities that match current operational needs.

We evaluated AI-based automation tools that target DevOps methodology and cloud-native solutions after performing research of their applications. AI-assisted monitoring systems enable high deployment speeds along with reduced downtime while simultaneously decreasing human mistakes in operations controlled by DevOps experts. The described capabilities both speed up application lifecycles and reduce system failure possibilities.

The group examined AI applications that function inside enterprise systems. These include the following:

Chatbots present real-time customer support systems in addition to providing real-time solutions for engagement.

The system uses this maintenance approach to detect upcoming failure patterns through examination of historical data patterns.

System activities together with security threats become detectable as anomalies by anomaly detection software which detects abnormal behavior patterns immediately.

The analysis included studies about security requirements while investigating scaling factors that impact the creation of AI-based solutions. The introduction of AI systems requires an organized system of personal data protection along with moral safeguards to comply with all applicable data laws, including GDPR and HIPAA.

Current technology deeply depends on AI because this technology constitutes an essential architectural element for developing modern software systems. Businesses achieve current delivery goals while making future predictions because predictive abilities were made possible through the integration process. Scalable intelligent applications together with resilient ones will combine artificial intelligence tools with cloud-native technologies and microservices foundation respectively.

The subsequent part discusses data pipeline management along with real-time analytics integration into optical system transformations to create advanced business intelligence for fast decision-making processes.

CHAPTER 10

Performance Optimization in Modern Applications

Introduction

Performance optimization is a critical aspect of modern application development. Ensuring an application runs efficiently, scales appropriately, and maintains high availability is essential for providing a seamless user experience. This chapter will cover:

- The importance of performance optimization in microservices and cloud applications.

- Identifying and resolving performance bottlenecks.

- Caching strategies for improved efficiency.

- Optimizing database performance.

- Leveraging load balancing and auto-scaling.

- Real-world examples and best practices.

© Mrinmoy Aich and Diganta Sengupta 2026
M. Aich and D. Sengupta, *Cloud-Native Modernization Unleashed,*
https://doi.org/10.1007/979-8-8688-2379-4_10

Understanding Performance Bottlenecks

Performance bottlenecks can arise at multiple layers of a modernized application—database, network, application logic, and underlying infrastructure. Identifying these issues early is essential for maintaining responsiveness and stability. The following are common bottleneck categories, along with practical tools and techniques used to diagnose them in real-world systems. Common performance issues include:

- **High CPU and Memory Usage**: Inefficient algorithms or excessive resource consumption.

  Inefficient algorithms, memory leaks, or unbounded data structures can push CPU and memory consumption beyond acceptable thresholds. In practice, teams often rely on profiling tools such as perf, top, htop, and VisualVM to understand which threads or functions are consuming the most resources. These tools provide visibility into garbage collection frequency, thread behavior, and hotspots within the code.

- **Slow Database Queries**: Poorly indexed databases, complex queries, or high latency.

  Poor indexing strategies, expensive joins, and high data volume can result in degraded database throughput. Most databases provide built-in profiling features— such as EXPLAIN, query analyzers, and slow-query logs—to help developers understand execution plans and identify missing indexes or suboptimal query patterns.

- **Network Latency**: Delays in communication between microservices.

  Communication delays between microservices or across regions can significantly impact the overall user experience. To pinpoint network-related issues, developers commonly use tools like tcp dump, Wireshark, or metrics from a service mesh (e.g., Istio, Linkerd). These provide insights into packet flow, connection retries, and latency distributions across services.

- **Concurrency Issues**: Thread contention and inefficient locking mechanisms.

  Microservices operating in high-traffic environments often encounter thread contention, deadlocks, or inefficient locking mechanisms. It's important to consider how thread pools, asynchronous tasks, and event-driven designs influence performance. A misconfigured thread pool can starve incoming requests, while blocking operations inside async workflows can degrade throughput. Proper sizing of thread pools and avoiding unnecessary synchronization are critical for maintaining concurrency efficiency.

Performance Bottlenecks in Modern Applications

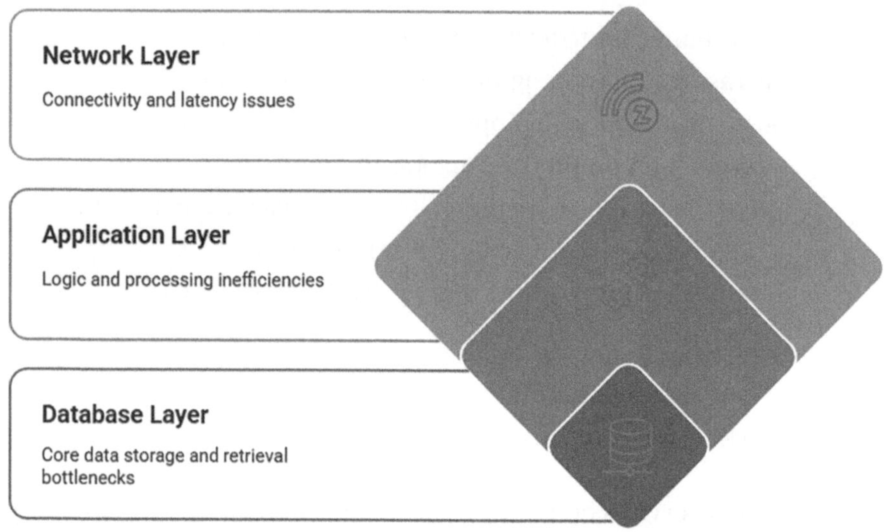

Figure 10-1. Performance Bottleneck Areas in a Modern Application (Diagram showcasing bottlenecks in database, application, and network layers.)

Caching Strategies for Performance Improvement

The method known as caching provides substantive benefits for lessening application runtime through temporary storage of popular data requests. The processes of data caching eliminate multiple data requests from primary sources, thus producing faster responses and minimizing backend utilization while delivering better user experience.

Caching is a fundamental performance technique used to reduce latency, lower database load, and improve overall system responsiveness. A well-designed system typically uses a multi-layered caching hierarchy, where each layer serves a different purpose depending on speed, cost, and distance from the application.

1. **L1 Cache—Local/In-memory Cache**
   What It Is:

   This is the closest cache to the application instance. It usually exists inside the application's memory space—for example, using ConcurrentHashMap, Caffeine, Guava Cache, or built-in framework caching.

   When to Use:

   Use L1 caching for high-frequency, read-heavy operations where ultra-low latency is important.

   Real-World Examples:

   - Caching user session details in a web server

   - Storing configuration values that are read often

   - Holding recently accessed product prices in an e-commerce backend

   Strengths:

   - Fastest response time (microseconds)

   - No network calls

   - Useful for per-instance decisions

   Limitations:

   - Not shared across multiple application nodes

   - Risk of stale data if not synchronized with other layers

2. **L2 Cache—Distributed Cache**

What It Is:

This is a shared cache accessible across multiple application instances, typically implemented using **Redis, Memcached, Hazelcast**, or similar systems.

When to Use:

Use L2 caching when you need **consistency across multiple servers** and want to reduce load on downstream systems.

Real-World Examples:

- Storing authentication tokens for distributed services

- Caching user profiles for microservices that run behind a load balancer

- Holding frequently accessed database query results

Strengths:

- Shared across nodes → consistent cache view

- Scales horizontally

- Reduces pressure on primary databases

Limitations:

- Slightly slower than L1 due to network hops

- Requires a cache invalidation strategy to prevent stale entries

3. **L3 Cache—Content Delivery Network (CDN)**

What It Is:

L3 caching sits at the network edge, closest to end users. CDNs like **Cloudflare**, **Akamai**, or **AWS CloudFront** cache static assets and sometimes dynamic API responses.

When to Use:

Use L3 caching for **static or semi-static content** that is accessed globally.

Real-World Examples:

- Images, CSS, JavaScript files for a website

- Product catalog pages for an e-commerce platform

- Cached API responses for public content (e.g., weather summaries)

Strengths:

- Lowest latency for global clients

- Reduces traffic to your origin servers

- Handles massive scale with minimal configuration

Limitations:

- Not suitable for rapidly changing transactional data

- Requires cache expiry and invalidation planning

Several widely implemented caching methods function in modern applications through the following list:

1. **In-memory Caching**

   Extremely fast data read and write operations are possible through memory caches that store data inside RAM. The widely used caching solutions are Redis and Memcached. Session-related information alongside user preferences along with common dataset items benefit most from using this caching technique. Popular technologies such as Redis and Memcached are widely used to store session details, user preferences, access tokens, configuration values, and shared dataset fragments that benefit from microsecond-level access times.

   Redis Single-Node vs. Redis Cluster for Scalability

   A single Redis instance is simple to operate and works well for moderate workloads, especially in applications where the dataset fits comfortably into the memory of one machine. However, as applications grow, a single node can become a bottleneck.

   Redis Cluster addresses these limitations by sharding data across multiple nodes.
   Key advantages include

   - **Scalability**: The dataset is distributed, allowing horizontal growth as data volume increases.

   - **High Availability**: Failover mechanisms ensure the cache continues operating even if a node fails.

   - **Better Throughput**: Read and write operations can be parallelized across shards.

A real-world scenario might involve an e-commerce platform where product catalog metadata needs to be cached. A single-node Redis might handle the load during early stages, but during large sales events, a Redis Cluster becomes essential to sustain request spikes and maintain low latency.

Cache Eviction Policies (LRU, LFU, TTL Considerations)

In-memory caches have finite RAM. When they reach capacity, they must evict entries to make space for new ones. Different policies influence how this happens:

LRU (Least Recently Used): Evicts the item that has not been accessed for the longest time.
Useful when recent access patterns are good predictors of future usage.

LFU (Least Frequently Used): Removes items that are accessed least often.
Effective for datasets where popularity matters—e.g., product pages or trending content.

TTL (Time-to-Live): Keys expire automatically after a defined period.
Ideal for session data, authentication tokens, or temporary feature flags.

Choosing the wrong policy can degrade cache performance. For example, an LFU policy may outperform LRU on an analytics dashboard where users repeatedly load the same few data widgets.

2. **Content Delivery Network (CDN) Caching**

   CDNs cache static content like images, videos, stylesheets, and scripts at edge locations closer to users. The location of data within optimum proximity to users greatly reduces their waiting time when accessing content from different parts of the world. The content caching solutions from Cloudflare and Akamai function at an advanced level for dynamic and static content storage.

   Dynamic Content Caching at the Edge

   Modern CDNs can store the results of API responses or dynamically generated pages for short periods. This helps reduce repeated load on backend systems while still maintaining acceptable freshness of the data.

   Examples of suitable use cases include:

   - Frequently accessed search results (e.g., "Top hotels in New Delhi this week").

   - Product recommendations that update every few minutes.

   - Regional content such as local weather summaries or pricing data.

   Instead of routing every request back to the origin server, the edge node can serve the cached dynamic response instantly, which improves responsiveness during traffic spikes.

   Cache Purging Strategies

   Because dynamic data changes more often than static assets, maintaining accuracy requires a deliberate purging strategy. CDNs provide several methods:

- **Key-Based Purge:** Remove a specific cached URL when related data changes (e.g., purging /api/hotel/123 when hotel 123 updates its pricing).

- **Event-Driven Purge:** Automatically purge content when updates occur in the CMS, database, or backend services—often via webhooks.

- **TTL-Based Expiry:** Set short-lived time-to-live values so dynamic content refreshes automatically without explicit purge commands.

- **Full Cache Invalidation:** Used sparingly, typically during deployments or major content updates.

  A well-designed purge strategy ensures that dynamic caching improves performance **without** serving outdated or inconsistent information.

3. **Database Query Caching**
   Companies implementing database caching preserve the output of costly queries and commonly executed SQL statements. The Hibernate second-level cache plus Redis serve as tools for result storage that eliminates reprocessing requirements.

4. **Application-Level Caching**
   Application frameworks supply built-in caching elements that developers can directly integrate with their business logic. Through the Spring Framework, developers can implement caching annotations, which enable them to create transparent method call result caching.

5. **HTTP Caching**

   The HTTP response caching function of browsers and proxies depends on the Cache-Control, ETag, and Expires configuration headers within the HTTP response. The system minimizes unneeded API requests, which results in better user experience by perceived performance improvement.

6. **Write-Through and Write-Behind Caching**

   The system writes data to the cache and database simultaneously through write-through caching. Data first goes into the cache before it continues asynchronously to the database storage.

   The different strategies fulfill distinct application requirements. Application requirements, together with consistency needs and data volatility, determine which caching technique should be selected. It is most effective to apply mixed caching strategies for optimal outcomes. Common caching strategies include the following.

In-memory Caching

The technique of in-memory caching uses system RAM to hold data that gets accessed often, which leads to extremely fast data read and write operations. In-memory storage defeats traditional disk systems because it gives high-performance access to stored data through its fast response times.

Tools: Redis, Memcached

Reset contains Redis and Memcached, which function as the two most common solutions for in-memory caching operations.

Redis:

The robust data structure system maintains strings and hashes as well as lists and sets in addition to other data types. The Redis tool provides systems with distributed features as well as pub/sub messaging and TTL policies and data persistence features.

Memcached:

The high-performance key-value store operates as an object caching solution to decrease database activity through memory object storage. The system offers lightweight performance with efficiency, but it does not contain the complete range of features Redis offers.

The application can benefit from storing its most sought-after data types in memory using this method.

Memory caching utilizes two common storage mechanisms which include:

Session data (e.g., user authentication tokens)

Read operations on databases happen often for product listings together with profile information.

API responses or computed results

City Cart Notifications and Shopping Cart Contents in e-commerce platforms

Example Scenario:

Thousands of customers on this e-commerce site continuously make product detail (name, price, stock) queries. Redis provides cache storage that reduces the need for database inquiries on these specific items.

Workflow:

The application system first searches product details inside Redis memory.

The system returns data immediately after finding it within the cache.

Database queries from the application take place when the cache contains no matching information (cache miss). The application then stores retrieved database results in Redis for upcoming requests.

The system results in lower database pressure while speeding up responses and making it more expandable.

Benefits of In-memory Caching:

Memory obtains data quicker than any disk I/O system.

The system uses this approach to decrease the number of necessary database requests.

Scalability: Supports high traffic without performance degradation.

Configuring TTLs enables automatic expiration of data stored in databases through memory flexibility.

Best Practices:

Establish a proper Time-to-Live setting that prevents data expiration.

The implementation of valid cache invalidation techniques is essential to keep data precise.

Observing the hit and miss rates from cache systems helps in optimizing performance.

Binary file storage in system memory is not recommended since it consumes extra storage capacity.

The method of storing data in memory remains critical for achieving performance optimization in modern software because it benefits particular applications involving microservices architectures along with real-time systems and high-traffic web platforms.

```java
// Example: Using Redis for caching in Spring Boot
@Bean
public RedisTemplate<String, Object> redisTemplate() {
    RedisTemplate<String, Object> template = new
    RedisTemplate<>();
    template.setConnectionFactory(redisConnectionFactory());
    return template;
```

Database Query Caching

Organizations keep operating legacy systems, yet these systems contain major security vulnerabilities that endanger their computer data and facilities. The applications started their development during a time when security standards and best practices were not common thus making them exposed to various cyber threats. The following list contains security risks that typically appear in legacy systems:

- Outdated authentication mechanisms

  Legacy applications insecurely authenticate users through three main methods, including direct password use, basic HTTP session passwords, and self-developed authentication systems that do not enforce security standards. Attacks happen easily due to these vulnerable security mechanisms that modern attackers can breach using brute-force and credential stuffing methods. Legacy systems remain unable to adopt the latest authentication methods, including multi-factor authentication (MFA) or OAuth 2.0 and SSO (Single Sign-On), since they cannot easily accommodate these secure standards.

- Lack of encryption

  Legacy systems normally store data as well as transmit it through unencrypted plain text formats. The absence of encryption makes sensitive information vulnerable to open access by attackers who can easily intercept it and gain unauthorized access to login credentials and personal data as well as financial details. Legacy applications reveal organizations to data breaches as well as compliance violations through their lack of encryption features during rest and transit operations. In these older environments, both the TLS protocol for data movement and the AES encryption standard for data storage often fail to appear.

- Hardcoded credentials

  Older applications frequently use original methods by placing authentication details directly into their source code base or configuration files. The practice results in major security risks since anyone who acquires access to the codebase and server will obtain those credentials. The persistent vulnerability exists because hard-coded credentials are not updated even though they remain accessible to intruders.

The absence of proper security measures transforms legacy systems into especially vulnerable targets for hackers. Security and compliance requirements need modern organizations to solve these problems as they prepare for the current threat environment and its long-term security needs.

Content Delivery Network (CDN)

- **Tools**: Cloudflare, AWS CloudFront.

- **Use Case**: Caching static assets like images, JavaScript, and CSS files.

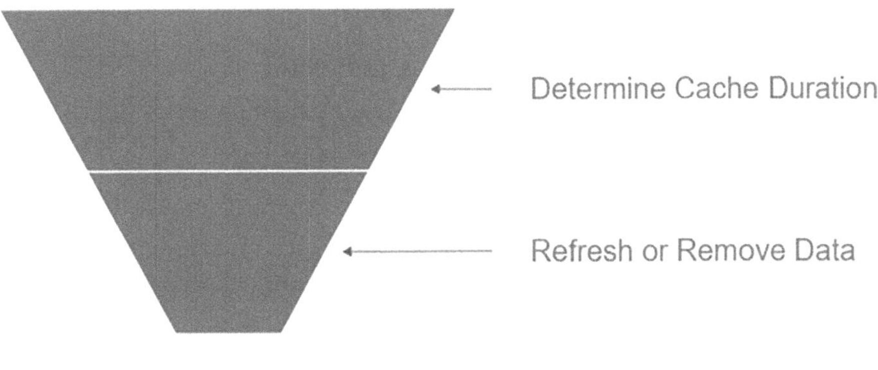

Figure 10-2. *Caching Strategy Flow*

Optimizing Database Performance

Databases often become a performance bottleneck. Strategies for optimization include:

Indexing

The system provides accelerated search functionality through its Use Case.

The database optimization strategy known as indexing creates indexes that develop data structures to support rapid database record retrieval from extensive data collections. The database index functions the same way an index works in a book by directing the system to rows without reading the complete table.

Index Maintenance and Trade-offs

While indexing significantly improves read performance, it also introduces operational trade-offs that developers must consider when designing a high-performance system. Indexes are not "free"—they require ongoing maintenance by the database engine.

A) **Impact on Inserts, Updates, and Deletes**

Every time a record is inserted, updated, or deleted, the database must also update its related index entries.

Insert operations:

When a new row is added, each index associated with the table must insert a new pointer.

For tables with many indexes, this can noticeably slow down bulk inserts or high-volume write workloads.

Update operations:

Updating an indexed column requires deleting the old index entry and creating a new one.

For frequently updated fields (e.g., product stock, order status), excessive indexing can create unnecessary overhead.

Delete operations:

Index entries pointing to the removed row must also be deleted.

This increases I/O work during cleanup operations.

Example:

An e-commerce order table with 8–10 indexes may deliver fast retrieval for analytics, but it will place a heavy load on write operations during peak ordering hours.

B) **Storage Cost**

Indexes consume additional disk space because each index stores a structured representation of table rows.

The more indexes a table has, the larger the overall storage footprint becomes.

- A B-tree index can sometimes grow to **30–50%** of the size of the base table.

- Composite indexes increase storage even further because they include multiple column values.

- Full-text indexes are often the largest and can exceed the size of the original text.

For cloud-hosted databases, this also affects **billing**, as storage is often charged by usage.

How It Works:

- Supplying an index allows the database engine to perform quick data retrieval, while a full table scan operation means scanning every row in the table. Database performance accelerates dramatically when users implement indices because they decrease the number of disk operations needed to load data.

Common Types of Indexes:

- The B-tree index functions as the default index in most relational databases, including MySQL and PostgreSQL, that provides rapid data access for ordered data structures.

- The Hash Index enables fast lookup of a particular key through equality searches.

- Such indexes contain data from multiple columns, which makes them effective when users filter their queries utilizing many columns simultaneously.

- The full-text index system enables large text searches in blog posts and documents.

- Spatial Index: Optimized for spatial/ geographic data.

Example:

- A table named `Products` contains thousands of entries with fields like `ProductID`, `Name`, `Category`, and `Price`.

Without Indexing:

- A search query like `SELECT * FROM Products WHERE Name = 'Wireless Mouse'` requires scanning the entire table.

With an Index on `Name`:

- The database can instantly jump to the matching rows, returning results in milliseconds.

```
CREATE INDEX idx_user_email ON users(email);
```

Query Optimization

- **Use Case**: Optimizing SQL queries for better performance.

Example:

```
EXPLAIN ANALYZE SELECT * FROM orders WHERE customer_
id = 123;
```

Connection Pooling

- **Tools**: HikariCP, C3P0.

- **Use Case**: Reusing database connections for efficiency.

Figure 10-3. *Database Performance Optimization Techniques*

Load Balancing and Auto-scaling

Load balancing and auto-scaling help distribute traffic efficiently and ensure application availability.

Load Balancing

- **Tools**: Nginx, HAProxy, AWS Elastic Load Balancer.

- **Use Case**: Distributing requests across multiple servers.

```
# Example: Load Balancing with Nginx
upstream backend_servers {
    server server1.example.com;
    server server2.example.com;
}
server {
    location / {
        proxy_pass http://backend_servers;
```

Auto-scaling

- **Tools**: AWS Auto Scaling, Kubernetes Horizontal Pod Autoscaler.

- **Use Case**: Dynamically adding or removing resources based on demand.

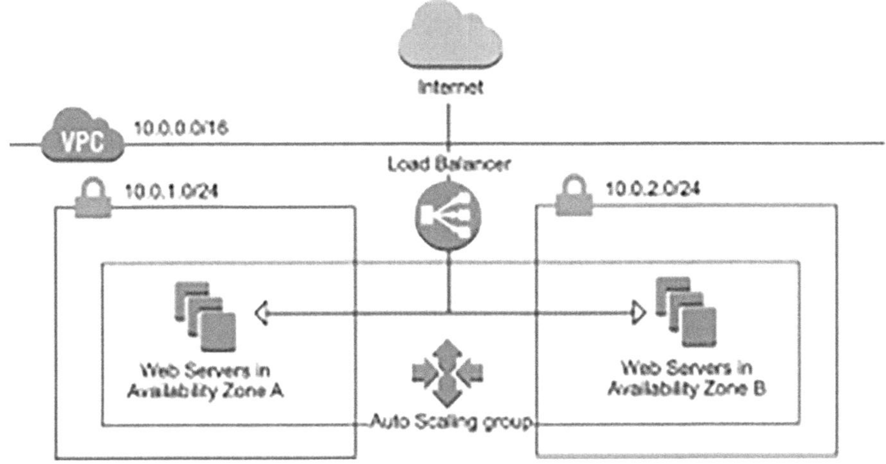

Figure 10-4. *Load Balancing and Auto-Scaling Workflow*

Real-World Performance Optimization Examples

Case Study: Optimizing a High-traffic E-commerce Application

- **Problem**: Slow response times during peak traffic

- **Solution**:

    - Implemented Redis caching

    - Optimized database queries

    - Used a CDN for static assets

    - Deployed Kubernetes auto-scaling

- **Result**: 50% improvement in page load time and reduced server costs

Case Study: Microservices Performance Tuning

- **Problem**: High network latency in service-to-service communication.

- **Solution**:

  - Implemented gRPC for faster communication.

  - Used circuit breakers with Resilience4j.

  - Optimized logging to reduce I/O overhead.

- **Result**: 40% reduction in latency.

Performance Optimization Process

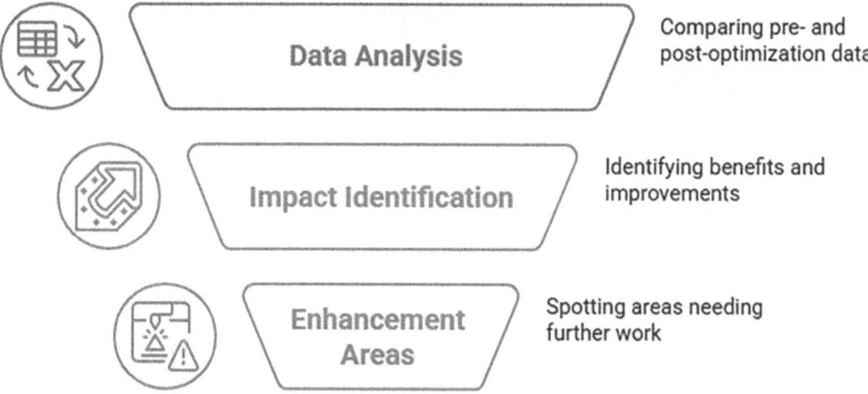

Figure 10-5. *Before and After Performance Optimization Metrics*

Best Practices for Performance Optimization

- **Use Asynchronous Processing**: Reduce blocking operations with message queues.

- **Optimize Logging and Monitoring**: Use ELK Stack, Prometheus, and Grafana.

- **Profile Applications**: Use tools like JProfiler, New Relic, and Datadog.

- **Implement Circuit Breakers**: Prevent cascading failures with Resilience4j.

- **Reduce API Payloads**: Use GraphQL or pagination to optimize API responses.

Conclusion

The chapter presents practical strategies and tested techniques for modern application performance improvement. Performance tuning exists as a complex method to ensure rapid application execution speed with adaptable features, system reliability, and uniform system response across various computing environments.

- We started our method by determining standard performance factors, which limit both system speed and application response durations. Three main defects responsible for poor performance involve inadequate programming combined with slow network systems and poor infrastructure.

- The research study evaluated two efficient database caching systems known as Redis and Memcached to examine their speedup capabilities, which decrease database query repetition. The update section concentrated on implementing index systems toward database query optimization, which made systems run faster.

- Our team performed a joint assessment of auto-scaling with load balancing systems because they enable design scalability and availability. The automated traffic management system and self-adjusting resource allocation maintain operational applications across different workload levels under essential performance conditions.

- During our implementation at the production level, we observed improvements because we enhanced API speed and removed external dependencies and asynchronous coding.

- The last part of the document presented best practices that incorporated APMs for performance monitoring and stress testing and performance benchmarking methodologies that would help prevent application failures during its operational lifetime.

Organizations can create applications that provide optimal performance and resilience through the implementation of these optimization methods at cost-effective operations. The next chapter illustrates principles for managing financial costs within cloud applications while maintaining performance quality together with availability.

CHAPTER 11

Introduction to Agentic AI in Application Modernization

Introduction

Modernizing legacy applications has become one of the most persistent challenges in enterprise IT. Large organizations—banks with decades-old COBOL systems, utilities operating brittle billing engines, or government agencies tied to mainframe workflows—often run software with tens of thousands of interdependent modules. These systems power mission-critical business operations, yet their complexity, undocumented behaviors, and operational fragility make modernization slow, risky, and heavily dependent on scarce human expertise. This is the context in which agentic AI enters—not to replace engineers, but to reduce human bottlenecks, accelerate safe modernization decisions, and provide continuous guardrails throughout the transformation journey.

© Mrinmoy Aich and Diganta Sengupta 2026
M. Aich and D. Sengupta, *Cloud-Native Modernization Unleashed*,
https://doi.org/10.1007/979-8-8688-2379-4_11

Traditional application modernization approaches have focused on breaking down monolithic systems and moving them to the cloud while creating APIs for legacy systems. The established modernization methods enhance scalability and maintainability yet require human involvement during discovery and refactoring and testing and deployment and governance steps. Through its implementation, agentic AI brings goal-oriented software agents that utilize tools to plan and act while learning and collaborating for complete modernization acceleration and risk reduction.

The implementation of agentic AI serves as a tool to enhance engineering judgment without functioning as a direct substitute. Through integration of architectural rules and compliance policies with documentation and tickets and code history, along with real-time data from CI/CD and observability agents, bounded tasks are performed autonomously, including proposing strangler-fig decompositions, validating refactoring patches, updating IaC, and running migration rehearsals before forwarding exceptions to human operators. Y - A memory and model: context windows, vector stores, or knowledge graphs for architecture and dependency knowledge; learning components to improve plans and action selection.

The organized application of goal-directed software agents, which utilize tools under defined policies, enables modernization task planning and execution and continuous lifecycle improvement according to the definition of agentic AI for modernization.

The Necessity of Agentic AI Stands As a Fundamental Requirement for Legacy Application Modernization

Legacy portfolios face a well-known set of obstacles that include tribal knowledge loss and outdated documentation.

Tight Coupling: risky refactors, hidden dependencies, and fragile test coverage.

Operational Risk: limited observability, unclear SLOs, and manual release steps.

Throughput Bottlenecks: change advisory boards, handoffs, and lengthy regression cycles.

Agentic AI implements solutions through five main approaches:

1. Modernization expertise codification through repeatable playbooks (e.g., strangler-fig, anti-corruption layer), which become executable agent strategies.

2. The automation of evidence creation happens through agents that generate diffs and tests along with performance baselines and rollback plans to enhance confidence and auditability.

3. Agents track repository changes and pipeline activities through continuous micro-migration proposals instead of conducting large-scale migrations.

4. The simulation of migrations in sandboxes by agents allows for SLO verification through synthetic checks before stopping operations on policy violations.

5. Economic advantages come from agents discovering and executing faster cycle times combined with lower rework and targeted cloud-cost optimization strategies including right-sizing and egress awareness.

Difference Between Traditional Automation and Agentic AI

Before diving into the dimensions, it helps to understand the core distinction: traditional automation executes tasks, whereas agentic AI decides what sequence of tasks should be executed to safely reach a goal.

Dimension	Traditional Automation	Agentic AI
Control model	Scripted, deterministic jobs	Goal-directed planning with adaptive steps
Scope	Fixed workflows (CI jobs, ETL tasks)	Open-ended tasks under constraints (plan, act, recover)
Context use	Narrow inputs; brittle to change	Broad context (code, tickets, metrics); resilient via tool use
Learning	None or offline tuning	Online/ongoing learning from outcomes and feedback
Coordination	Human-orchestrated	Multi-agent negotiation and role-based collaboration
Safety	Guarded by environment (e.g., RBAC)	Guarded by explicit policies, simulations, and human-in-the-loop

Traditional automation performs predefined steps, while agentic AI makes independent decisions about action sequences that accomplish goals within your safety limits.

Key Concepts of Agentic AI for Modernization

Autonomous Agents: Roles in Modernized Applications

To make these roles easier to understand, it is helpful to group them into the natural phases of a modernization initiative. Discovery agents map the system; planner agents define the strategy, refactor agents apply changes, test/security agents validate safety, and SRE/compliance agents control deployment and governance. Figure 11.x visualizes this flow and the handoff between agents across these phases.

- Modernization programs avoid using one all-knowing agent as their primary choice. Different agents with specific responsibilities must be created through a process of defining their duties and establishing handoff procedures. The following roles represent standard positions:

- **The Discovery Agent (Cartographer)**: It performs repository scans while analyzing build configurations and service catalogs and runtime telemetry to create domain maps and dependency graphs and identify hotspots, which are high churn plus high incident rate areas. The output consists of architecture diagrams as well as proposed modernization targets.

- **The Planner Agent (Architect)**: It chooses patterns between strangler-fig and event-driven decoupling and façade and database-per-service while organizing work into safe steps that produce acceptance criteria and KPIs.

- **Refactor Agent (Developer):** It produces patches including API extractions together with interface adapters and updates to configurations and IaC while recommending tests. The agent functions exclusively within feature branches along with ephemeral environments.

- **Test Engineer Agent (Quality):** It develops contract tests and maintains regression suites while creating performance smoke/load tests alongside resilience probes and coverage reports which match risk levels.

- **Security Agent (AppSec):** It executes SCA/SAST/DAST scans and threat model comparisons while enforcing security policies and providing remediation recommendations.

- **SRE Agent (Operations):** It generates new runbooks and updates existing ones while creating SLOs and alert systems and synthetic monitoring checks; it performs validation of canary deployment procedures including rollback processes.

- **Compliance Agent (Governance):** It verifies that all audit trails and SoD requirements alongside regulatory constraints are met before creating evidence packs.

Agent Task Contract (Example)

task: "Extract and externalize billing calculations from monolith to service"
   constraints:

- "Read-only in prod; write in feature branch only"

- "All changes must pass contract tests and perf smoke"

- "Security policy P-123: no secrets in code; SBOM generated" success_criteria:

- "p95 latency $\leq$ baseline + 10%"

- "Change Failure Rate does not increase over 2 sprints"

- "All modified endpoints backward compatible"

review:

- "Human code review required for public API changes"

tools:

- analyzers: [dep-graph, call-graph, linter]

- ci: [pipeline-api]

- tests: [contract, perf-smoke]

- infra: [iac-engine]

Multi-agent Systems Coordinating Microservices

Modernized estates typically adopt micro services or modular architectures.

Multi-agent systems mirror this structure:

- The critical services maintain their own local agents that possess complete understanding of service codebases and deployment topologies and SLOs and contracts.

- A top-level agent functions as an orchestrator to direct service-wide modifications and handle conflict resolution between agents while managing their negotiation processes.

- All agents share access to a knowledge graph or vector store, which stores API schemas along with dependency graphs and decision logs and policy artifacts.

- Agents communicate through standardized messages, which include propose, critique, revise, and approve sequences that produce traceable conversation logs.

Typical multi-agent workflow for a schema change:

1. The Planner initiates a versioned API proposal which contains a deprecation timeline.

2. The Refactor Agents that represent producers and consumers create updated code versions.

3. Test Engineer Agent updates contract tests; SRE Agent prepares canary and synthetic probes.

4. Compliance Agent verifies policy and evidence; Orchestrator gates rollout based on tests and SLO impact.

Pattern: Event-first collaboration. Agents first implement event streams (outbox or CDC) to decrease synchronous dependencies before performing caller migration steps.

The orchestrator implements explicit failure management by stopping operations when policies fail, then creating *incident* reports with difference files, followed by Git-based reversion and human owner notification through paging systems.

Self-learning Capabilities for Evolving Application Workflows

These agentic systems are improved over time through feedback loops:

Outcome Learning: Agents observe task outcomes (success, rollback, incident) and update their priors for the strategy; for instance, to prefer the adapter pattern over large-scale interface changes in cases of low coverage.

The learning loop is one of the most important properties of agentic systems. Instead of performing tasks blindly, agents continuously incorporate feedback from test results, incidents, rollbacks, and human review. This turns modernization into a self-improving cycle rather than a one-off project.

- **Reward Shaping**: Rewards are defined against modernization KPIs—cycle time reduction, escaped defect rate, cost savings, and SLO adherence—so that agents optimize for business value, rather than mere completion of tasks.

- **Policy Aware Exploration**: Exploration is limited to sandboxes or canary stages, wherein policies set maxima on the blast radius.

- **Data Sources for Learning**: Code diffs, test results, performance baselines, production telemetry, incident postmortems, and human reviews provide top-notch training signals.

- **Knowledge Consolidation**: Promoted learnings become playbook entries or rules (e.g., "When migrating JVM services to containers, apply JVM flags X/Y and increase readiness probe delay").

Practice Tip: First, with hawk-eyed scrutiny, the data is gathered offline from real-life incident repos and fake ones, i.e., from the mishaps and the hyped-up incidents of the day. Then, it moves to online learning once everything is checked about the policy gates and rollback reliability.

Benefits of Agentic AI in Cloud Native Modernized Applications

Enterprises that have piloted agentic AI report measurable improvements. A typical modernization cycle that took 2–3 weeks from proposal to deployment now completes in 2–3 days. Escaped defects fall from 12% to under 4%, and CFR decreases by 20–40% across the first three sprints. Cloud native allows platforms (containers, serverless, and service meshes) to go beyond maximizing the agentic benefits by providing a single front-end API, an elastic environment, and rich observability:

- **Speed to Value**: Agents spin up ephemeral migration rehearsal environments, smoke-test performance rapidly, and tear them down, thus compressing feedback loops form days to minutes.

- **Risk Reduction**: Canary, feature flags, and automated rollback reduce blast radius. Agents consider real SLOs and error budgets in determining rollout speed.

- **Quality and Reliability**: Continuous updating and generation of contract testing and synthetic probing; CFR and MTTR rates decline thanks to fixes institutionalized by agents.

- **Cost Efficiency**: Right sizing, autoscaling policies, and storage tiering along with data egress optimizations are recommended by Agents; actions are executed with IaC having approvals.

- Security and compliance include SBOM generation, dependency upgrades, secret scanning, and policy checks pushed into a continuous evidence-backed process.

- **Documentation That Is Fresh**: With every change, architecture views, runbooks, and ADRs get generated by agents, so there is no drift.

Getting Started: A Practical Adoption Path

Most enterprises cannot adopt all agentic capabilities at once. A safe, incremental path is recommended:

1. Start with the Discovery Agent to build an accurate dependency map and hotspot analysis.

2. Add the Planner Agent to generate modernization proposals and acceptance criteria.

3. Enable sandboxed Refactor and Test Agents to perform safe, reversible actions with full policy gating.

4. Gradually adopt Security, SRE, and Compliance Agents once confidence in the guardrails has been established.

5. Introduce multi-agent orchestration only after individual agents prove reliable.

This progressive approach aligns with real enterprise risk patterns and ensures trust in the system develops naturally.

A Quick Illustrative Scenario

A North American energy utility faced a 6-week cycle time for even minor modernization changes due to complex review and testing pipelines. After introducing discovery, planning, and test-automation agents, their cycle time dropped to 10 days, with CFR improving by 35%. This allowed the organization to modernize high-risk modules without increasing operational risk.

Legacy billing monolith → event-driven microservice

1. Discovery Agent maps a dense dependency cluster around billing calculations and flags high change failure rate.

2. Planner Agent selects the strangler-fig pattern with an anti-corruption layer and versioned events.

3. Refactor Agent extracts the calculation logic behind a new interface, generates adapter code, and updates IaC for the containerized service.

4. Test Engineer Agent writes contract tests and performs smoke tests for performance; Security Agent validates SBOM and policies.

5. SRE Agent writes SLO, canary plan, and synthetic probes. The Orchestrator coordinates the rollout; Compliance Agent assembles an evidence pack.

6. Outcome telemetry indicates p95 latency is +6% (within budget), and CFR is down over two sprints; learnings become part of the playbook in similar domains.

Governance and Safety (Cross-cutting)

- **Bounded Autonomy**: Agents must have defined boundaries for where they may act (environments, repos, services) and where they may only propose.

- **Human-in-the-Loop**: Approval must be granted for any changes to the public API, migrations of data, and policy exceptions.

- **Observability**: Every agent action must be trackable (indicating who did what and why), linking back to associated diffs, tests, and metrics.

- **Ethics and Compliance**: Data minimization, PII handling, regulatory limits must be respected; agents need to be policy-aware by design.

Metrics That Matter (For Chapter 11 Adoption)

- Cycle time from proposal → merged PR → verified deploy

- Change Failure Rate and MTTR post modernization

- Escaped defect rate (per release) and SLO adherence

- Coverage of modernization backlog (items closed per sprint)

- Cost KPIs: infra cost per transaction, egress, storage

Key Takeaway

- Agentic AI elevates modernization from scripted tasks to goal seeking, policy constrained action.

- Agents are assigned roles, with an orchestrator coordinating between role-based agents. Therefore, the microservice boundaries are reflected, and coordination risk is decreased.

- First, read use for discovery and planning. Then, enqueue bounded write actions within sandboxes with strong rollback guarantees.

- Learn from business outcomes—CFR, MTTR, SLOs, and cost—thus, empowering such agents that optimize for value instead of vanity metrics.

- Cloud-native platforms enhance agent benefits by providing ephemeral environments, observability, and uniform APIs.

In the upcoming chapters, we will convert these in theory into actual reference architectures, implementation patterns, and adoption roadmaps with guardrails and KPIs.

CHAPTER 12

Identifying Modernization Workflows Suitable for Agentic AI

Introduction

Not every modernization effort can be the aspiration of the autonomous agent, and not every legacy impediment can be safely delegated to autonomous agency agents. The choice is made for those workflows wherein agentic AI can provide outsized leverage—threats large but patterned code bases, with risks containable by policy; and measurable outputs-cycle time, change-fail rate, SLO adherence, cost—that can be improved through the tool-assisted intervention ad infinitum. This chapter will act as the on-field guide in locating those workflows and preparing them for the oversight of the agent.

We will (1) assess legacy bottlenecks with an exacting and repeatable rubric, (2) map monolithic modules to agent-aligned microservices, (3) prioritize important workflows for autonomous optimization, and (4) tie agents into event-driven architectures (EDA), thus affording agents observation, decision, and action with minimal coupling and maximum safety. By then, you'll have a shortlist of high-value workflows that are ready for agents, coupled with the operationalization patterns.

Assessing Legacy Application Bottlenecks

Modernization of applications will succeed or fail with bottlenecks about knowledge, coupling, controls, and flow. Agentic AI is most useful when those bottlenecks are repetitive, diagnosable, and fixable with codes, tests, or infrastructure changes. Use the below seven-signal assessment to measure in which areas agents can have the greatest impact.

Signal 1: Customer Visible Friction

How directly does the poor quality or late delivery of a component affect users? Look for:

- High incident rate or change failure rate (CFR) hitting revenue-critical journeys (signup, payment, onboarding).

- Spike in VOC/CSAT/complaints correlated with specific modules or endpoints.

- Latency or reliability regression correlated with code churn. Agent leverage: agents generate contract tests for brittle endpoints, synthesize probes that simulate top complaints, and enforce performance smoke gates.

Signal 2: Inefficiency of the Flow in the Value Stream

Where does delivery time get wasted? Gather lead time data from issue trackers and CI/CD according to:

- Long waits on manual regression test cycles

- Frequent rework stemming from ambiguous
  requirements or missing test fixtures

- Hand-offs between teams for minor changes

Agent leverage: test-generating agents, environment-seeding agents, and planner agents that convert ambiguous tickets into executable acceptance criteria.

Signal 3: Structural Coupling and Code Health

Agents shine where there are seams and patterns that repeat. Indicators:

- High afferent/efferent coupling between packages;
  tangled imports; cyclic dependencies.

- Large classes or god modules; copy-paste variants of
  the same algorithm.

- Low test coverage paired with predictable interface
  patterns (e.g., REST + ORM). Agent leverage: refactor
  agents, extract interfaces, add anti-corruption layers,
  and generate adapters; test agents scaffold contract and
  mutation tests.

Signal 4: Data Gravity and Transaction Boundaries
Data shape decomposition. Watch for:

- Shared tables across domains; cross-cutting
  transactions; trigger webs.

- Heavy read/write hotspots; batch jobs contend
  with online flows. Agent leverage: agents propose
  outbox/CDC patterns, shard hot tables, and simulate
  consistency impacts through canary loads.

Signal 5: Observability and Testability

Agents need feedback. You are ready when:

- Trace/metric/logging on a basic level exists anywhere at service/module boundaries.

- Integration tests are deterministic, and datasets are seedable. Agent leverage: agents automatically expand probes, attach golden signals to change plans, and fail builds when telemetry is missing.

Signal 6: Risk and Compliance Surface

The next agent autonomy can be fostered when guardrails are explicit:

- Explicit policies (e.g., "no PII in logs," "SBOM required," "encryption in transit/at rest").

- RBAC segmented environments: dev, test, staging, and prod. Agent leverage: Compliance agents put policy into executable checks to create evidence packs and block violations via drift remediation.

Signal 7: Operations Toil and Cost Hotspots

Repetitive toil and cost anomalies can be targeted for automation:

- Manual restarts, noisy alarms, flapping autoscalers, expensive egress, or storage tiers. Agent leverage: SRE agents recommend and implement right sizing, alert hygiene, and autoscaling policies via IaC under approval gates.

The Bottleneck Discovery Pipeline

Operationalize the seven signals by a discovery pipeline:

1. **Ingest**: Repositories, build manifests, deployment descriptors, tickets, incident postmortems, observability metrics, and cost reports.

2. **Compute**: Churn, dependency centrality, CFR, MTTR, test gap index (critical endpoints without contract tests), telemetry completeness, policy breach counts, and cost per transaction.

3. **Correlate**: Overlay customer impact with structural risk (e.g., a frequently changing payment module with low testability is a high priority).

4. **Visualize**: Produce the heatmap by module/service, with red being the highest leverage potential by agents.

5. **Propose**: The agents (or your team) create variations of intervention with confidence scores and expected shift on KPI.

Practice Tip: Start with read-only agents that generate heatmaps and proposals; enable write privileges only for top-ranked, low-blast-radius modules.

Readiness Rubric (Scorecard)

Score each module from 1 (poor) to 5 (excellent) across the criteria below. **Agentic Readiness = Impact × (Seams + Feedback + Guardrails)**, where Impact is the average of Customer Friction and Flow Inefficiency scores.

Criterion	1	3	5
Customer Friction	Minimal user impact	Periodic minor impact	Direct revenue/ experience impact
Flow Inefficiency	Smooth flow	Occasional delays	Chronic delays and rework
Seams (Coupling/ Modularity)	God classes, cycles	Some interfaces exist	Clear seams; adapters viable

(*continued*)

Criterion	1	3	5
Feedback (Observability/ Testability)	Sparse logs, no tests	Basic metrics and tests	Tracing, SLOs, contract tests
Guardrails (Policy/ RBAC)	No clear policy	Partial policies	Enforced gates, evidence
Data Complexity	Cross-domain transactions	Some shared tables	Clear ownership; CDC feasible
Toil/Cost Hotspots	None	Moderate	Significant toil/cost anomalies

A typical first wave targets modules with **Impact ≥ 4** and **(Seams + Feedback + Guardrails) ≥ 10**.

Worked Example: Payments Module

- CFR 18%, MTTR 7h, low contract tests, observable 3/5, strong RBAC. **Readiness: High.**

- Agent plan: add contract tests, extract idempotency adapter, implement outbox, generate canary probes, and enforce perf smoke. **Expected**: CFR ↓ by 30–50%, MTTR ↓ by 25–40%.

Mapping Monolithic Modules to Microservices for Agentic Oversight

Agents operate best where responsibilities are crisp. The goal isn't microservices for their own sake; it's **cohesive, governable units** that agents can analyze, test, and deploy within safe autonomy envelopes.

Step 1: Domain Discovery and Candidate Boundaries

Use semantic code search, commit history, and runtime traces to surface natural **bounded contexts** (e.g., Billing, Catalog, Identity). Align with business capabilities and data ownership. Produce a **context map** showing dependencies and anti-corruption needs.

Step 2: Dependency Graph and Change Churn

Build a weighted call/dependency graph enriched with change frequency (commits/week) and defect density. Hotspots (high centrality × high churn) become prime candidates for protective facades or extraction.

Step 3: Transaction Boundary Analysis

Identify operations that must be atomic. If a module spans multiple domains within one transaction, prefer **sagas** or event-driven choreography over distributed transactions. Agents can draft candidate sagas and verify compensations in sandboxes.

Step 4: Data Seams and Strangler Routes

Locate seams where **outbox** or **change-data-capture (CDC)** can bridge old and new. Define immutable events (e.g., PaymentAuthorized, InvoiceIssued) with versioned schemas. Agents can scaffold outbox tables, producers, and consumers with idempotency keys.

Step 5: Interface Contracts and Backward Compatibility

Express proposed service contracts in OpenAPI/AsyncAPI. Generate **consumer-driven contract tests** and enforce compatibility with CI gates. Agents keep a **schema registry** current and fail builds on breaking changes without deprecation windows.

Step 6: Decomposition Backlog

Convert the map into a sequenced backlog:

- **Phase 1**: Façade and adapters to reduce blast radius.

- **Phase 2**: Extract high-value endpoints behind the façade.

- **Phase 3**: Migrate data ownership and retire legacy paths. Agents plan, generate diffs, and produce evidence for each phase.

Agent Oversight Topology

For each target service or module, assign roles:

- **Service Agent**: Local expert on code and tests; proposes refactors, generates patches.

- **Test Agent**: Maintains contracts, regression, and perf smoke.

- **Security Agent**: Enforces SBOM, secrets, and vulnerability SLAs.

- **SRE Agent**: SLOs, alerts, canary plans, and rollback runbooks.

- **Orchestrator**: Coordinates cross-service changes and policy gates.

Agent Task Graph (ATG)—Example

```
goal: "Externalize billing calculations"
nodes:
discover: {agent: service, outputs: [dep_graph, hotspots]}
plan: {agent: orchestrator, inputs: [dep_graph], outputs:
[change_plan]}
refactor: {agent: service, inputs: [change_plan], outputs:
[patches]}
test: {agent: test, inputs: [patches], outputs: [contracts,
perf_smoke]}
security: {agent: security, inputs: [patches], outputs:
[sbom, vulns]}
deploy: {agent: sre, inputs: [contracts, perf_smoke], outputs:
[canary_report]}
edges:
- discover -> plan -> refactor -> test -> security -> deploy
policies:
approvals: [public_api_change: human]
rollback: auto_on: [sla_breach, error_rate>1%]
```

Decomposition Antipatterns to Avoid

- **Nanoservices** without clear ownership—agents over-optimize and increase coordination cost.

- **Shared databases** post-split—breaks autonomy and complicates agent decisions.

- **Hidden sync coupling** through shared libraries—prefer versioned APIs or events.

Prioritizing Critical Processes for Autonomous Optimization

You will surface many candidate workflows; not all deserve immediate agent investment. Use a **portfolio view** with an explicit scoring model.

The RICE-A Model (Reach, Impact, Confidence, Effort, Autonomy Readiness)

- **Reach**: Transactions/users affected per period

- **Impact**: Expected KPI improvement (CFR, MTTR, latency, cost)

- **Confidence**: Quality of evidence supporting the estimate

- **Effort**: Human + compute time to enable agent oversight (tests, telemetry, policies)

- **Autonomy Readiness (A)**: Maturity of seams, feedback, and guardrails (from the section "Assessing Legacy Application Bottlenecks")

Score = (Reach × Impact × Confidence × A) / Effort.

Rank workflows by score and pick a **balanced set**: at least one quick win (low effort, moderate impact) and one strategic bet (high impact with medium effort). Document assumptions; let agents update the scores as telemetry arrives.

Define the Autonomy Envelope

Autonomy is not binary; it expands with trust.

1. **Observe**: Agents read artifacts and propose.

2. **Propose**: Agents generate plans, diffs, and tests; humans approve.

3. **Execute in Sandbox**: Agents run migrations/tests in ephemeral envs.

4. **Supervised Execution**: Controlled changes in staging/canary with auto-rollback.

5. **Steady-State Autonomy**: Agents operate within policy (e.g., nonbreaking dependency bumps, rotating secrets, regenerating tests) without human pre-approval.

Tie each workflow's autonomy envelope to **explicit policies** (what, where, when) and **rollback reliability** (mean rollback time, failure rate).

Example Portfolio Snapshot

- **Payments—Contract Testing and Idempotency**: Score 84 (Quick win). Autonomy Level: 4 (Supervised Execution).

- **Catalog—Search Relevance Tuning**: Score 58 (Strategic bet). Autonomy Level: 3 (Sandbox): requires offline evaluation harness.

- **Identity—Secret Rotation and SBOM Maintenance**: Score 72 (Operational hygiene). Autonomy Level: 5 (Steady state) with tight policy.

Connecting Agentic AI to Event-Driven Architecture

Events ➤ Agents ➤ Actions ➤ Measured Outcomes (Chapter 11) ➤ Feedback

Domain events (business facts) ➤ Service/Test agents ➤ Refactors, adapters, contract/perf tests ➤ CFR, lead time, latency/SLOs ➤ Updated change plans

Operational events (deploys/errors) ➤ SRE agent ➤ Canary/rollback, autoscaling, alert hygiene ➤ MTTR, SLO error-budget burn ➤ Safer autonomy envelope

Governance events (policy checks) ➤ Security/Compliance agent ➤ SBOM, secrets scanning, evidence packs ➤ Policy-breach rate, audit readiness ➤ Stronger guardrails

Learning signals (experiment results) ➤ Orchestrator agent ➤ Re-score RICEA, prioritize backlog ➤ Throughput/cost per transaction ➤ Continuous portfolio tuning

Mini-case Examples (Pros/Cons of Agentic Intervention):

Mini-case 1: Payments API schema evolution: When a PaymentAuthorized event version changes, the Test Agent can auto-generate consumer-driven contract tests and a compatibility report. Pros: faster regression coverage and fewer breaking releases; Cons: requires a disciplined schema registry and can appear noisy if consumers lack deterministic fixtures.

Mini-case 2: Flapping autoscaler and noisy alarms: Operational events (error spikes, high CPU, repeated restarts) can trigger an SRE Agent to propose right-sizing and alert deduplication via IaC. Pros: reduces toil and improves MTTR; Cons: guardrails must prevent unsafe production writes without canary validation and fast rollback.

Mini-case 3: Policy drift on PII logging: Governance events can trigger a Security Agent to block builds when log payloads violate the "no PII"

policy and to generate an evidence pack. Pros: continuous compliance and faster audits; Cons: false positives can slow delivery unless policies are tuned and exceptions are explicitly managed.

Agents thrive in **event-rich** systems. Events provide the senses and the levers agents need—observing state transitions, asserting invariants, and triggering actions without deep synchronous coupling.

Event Taxonomy for Modernization

- **Domain Events**: Business facts (e.g., PaymentCaptured). Immutable, versioned.

- **Operational Events**: Deploys, errors, SLO breaches, and cost anomalies.

- **Governance Events**: Policy evaluations, approvals, and evidence pack creation.

- **Learning Signals**: Experiment outcomes, rollback reasons, postmortem tags.

Event Design Principles

- **Immutability and Idempotency**: Include eventId, aggregateId, and occurredAt. Consumers must handle duplicates and reordering.

- **Schema Governance**: Registry with compatibility rules; deprecations carry timelines.

- **PII Minimization**: Use tokens or references; enforce data handling policies at the bus level.

- **Backpressure and DLQs**: Define retry, backoff, and dead-letter policies per topic.

AsyncAPI Snippet—PaymentAuthorized v2

```
asyncapi: "2.6.0"
info: {title: Payments, version: "2.0.0"}
```

```
channels:
payment.authorized.v2:
subscribe:
message:
name: PaymentAuthorized
payload:
type: object
required: [eventId, occurredAt, paymentId, amount, currency]
properties:
eventId: {type: string}
occurredAt: {type: string, format: date-time}
paymentId: {type: string}
amount: {type: number}
currency: {type: string}
metadata: {type: object}
```

Agent Subscriptions and Actions

Agents subscribe to events that match their mandate and policies.

Agent Policy—Contract Test Agent

```
subscribe:
- channel: payment.authorized.v2
filter: {schemaChange: true}
actions:
- generate_consumer_tests: {services: [checkout, refunds]}
- run_pipeline: {pipelineId: "contracts-ci"}
guardrails:
- max_runtime: "10m"
- environments: [sandbox, staging]
- approvals:
- type: human
when: [public_api_change]
```

```
evidence:
- upload: [test_reports, coverage, diffs]
notify:
- channel: "#modernization-agents"
```

CDC and Outbox Patterns for Legacy Bridges

For brownfield estates, let the monolith continue writing to its database while an **outbox** table captures domain events atomically. An agent:

1. Detects schema changes and updates the outbox mapper.

2. Validates event delivery and consumer lag.

3. Fails safe on mismatches, opening an incident with precise diffs.

For databases where CDC is available, agents manage connector configs, partitioning, and schema evolution; they also enforce **PII redaction** and **field-level encryption** policies at the stream processor.

Orchestration vs. Choreography

- Use **orchestration** (a saga orchestrator) where compensations are complex or cross-team coordination is fragile; the orchestrator can be an agent with policy-bound commands.

- Use **choreography** where services are loosely coupled and domain events suffice; agents validate invariants via synthetic transactions and probes.

Observability of the Event Mesh

Agents rely on **mesh observability:**

- Topic-level SLIs (publish latency, consumer lag, DLQ rates).

- Schema evolution dashboards.

- End-to-end tracing that links a code change ➤ event emission ➤ downstream SLO impact. Agents surface drifts (e.g., unconsumed events, orphan producers) and propose cleanups with safe migrations.

Security and Compliance on the Bus

- AuthN/Z for producers/consumers; per-topic RBAC.

- Content scanning for secrets; PII classification tags.

- Retention policies tied to data classification. Agents codify and enforce these as **pre-flight checks** before enabling new producers/consumers.

Summary

Link to Chapter 11 metrics: The workflows in this chapter should be governed using the same operational measures defined in Chapter 11— change failure rate (CFR), mean time to recovery (MTTR), lead time for changes, deployment frequency, SLO attainment/error-budget burn, and cost per transaction. In practice, each agent action (e.g., generating contract tests, proposing strangler routes, adjusting autoscaling policies, enforcing SBOM/PII gates) should emit telemetry that explicitly attributes deltas in these metrics to the change, enabling closed-loop learning: observe ➤ propose ➤ execute (under policy) ➤ measure ➤ refine.

Agentic AI delivers maximum value when pointed at **high-impact, repeatable, and governable** workflows. By scoring legacy modules on customer friction, flow inefficiency, structural seams, feedback quality, guardrails, data gravity, and toil/cost hotspots, you can build an **evidence-based shortlist** for agent oversight. Map monolith modules to **cohesive microservices** that reflect domain boundaries and data ownership; assign agent roles and policies to each. Prioritize through a transparent portfolio model (RICE-A) and evolve autonomy in stages—from observe to steady-state—anchored by rollback reliability.

Finally, connect agents to an **event-driven architecture** so they can observe state changes, coordinate safely, and leave a verifiable audit trail. With events as the fabric, agents learn from outcomes, close the loop on quality and cost, and keep modernization moving at a sustainable, measurable pace.

CHAPTER 13

Data Modernization and Migration Strategies

Introduction

As data architectures evolve, it is important to keep pace with changing requirements. This allows organizations to freely adopt new systems and scale effectively. In a business context, having a modernized data infrastructure is essential. The infrastructure should not just include a cloud migration of legacy systems or updated databases. It should incorporate a data modernization strategy that covers the evolution of data capture, storage, and utilization systems. As the dependency on data continues to grow in shaping business strategies, it is essential to evolve data structures. This chapter outlines the fundamental approaches and data migration and modernization considerations with a special focus on the data migration frameworks, tools, and processes that succeed in the current technological context.

© Mrinmoy Aich and Diganta Sengupta 2026
M. Aich and D. Sengupta, *Cloud-Native Modernization Unleashed*,
https://doi.org/10.1007/979-8-8688-2379-4_13

Data modernization strategies have a bigger picture rather than a purely technical one. They require constant data review and involve the entire business. AI and machine learning are becoming part of the data migration ecosystem, enabling the transformation of rigid, rule-based methods into self-optimizing systems. A company that adopts modern data methods stands to gain a lot more—both in operational efficiency and in overall data system agility and resilience. In this chapter, we will further discuss the necessity of a data migration strategy, the challenges these strategies face, and the approach to tackle these challenges in successful modernization.

Key business and technical benefits of data modernization include:

- Operational efficiency: faster provisioning, reduced maintenance overhead, and fewer manual data handoffs.

- Scalability and agility: elastic compute/storage, rapid experimentation, and easier system evolution.

- Support for AI/ML initiatives: improved data quality, lineage, and feature availability for model training and serving.

Added.

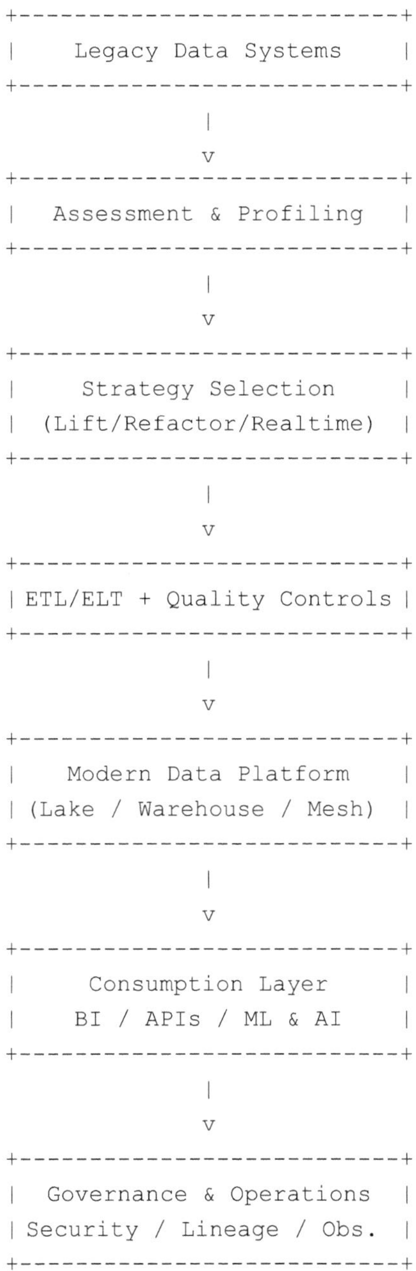

Figure 13-1. *Data Modernization Lifecycle (conceptual)*

Examining the Issues with Old Data Systems

The issues emanating from the old data systems make modernization all the more difficult. The technologies that existed a long time ago and the systems built with them tend to not work well with data still in use today. Some of the issues are as follows:

1. **Data Silos**: As a result of the legacy systems, data is stored in silos, which makes it a challenge to retrieve, update, or integrate it with data from other sources. This creates serious hurdles in the analytics process.

2. **Outdated Data Structures**: Data schemas tend to get rigid and less adaptive as time goes by. Without proper and cautious planning, refactoring or transforming these outdated structures can disrupt important processes.

3. **Incompatible Formats**: Moving data to modern systems that rely on open formats or cloud-native solutions is made difficult because of proprietary or outdated formats maintained by legacy systems.

4. **Knowledge Decay**: Older systems are impacted by knowledge decay, with crucial documentation either being outdated or not in existence. This lack of transparency leads to problems for teams dealing with the data modernization.

5. **Scalability Issues**: Legacy data systems often lack proper scalability, therefore restricting the efficient scaling of the organization's data infrastructure to satisfy growing needs.

With the knowledge of these challenges, a company is better equipped to plan the transition and steer clear of the common issues that come with legacy data systems.

Data Assessment and Profiling

Data assessment and profiling are critical preliminary activities in the data modernization cycle. Each organization should first explore data structure and quality in legacy systems prior to data migration and transformation.

Data assessment encapsulates the evaluation of the present data setup of an enterprise. Important facets include:

1. **Data Quality**: Does the data in question maintain accuracy, is it complete, and is it consistent? Inaccurate data, amongst others, can cause a ripple effect of data quality problems later on.

2. **Data Dependencies**: In older systems, there tend to be complex relations between data sources. Understanding and mapping out these dependencies is critical in understanding how to minimize risk during the system relocation.

3. **Data Volume and Growth**: The quantity of existing data, along with its growth rate and the processing or analysis speed, must be evaluated. This data informs decisions on cloud storage, data processing pipelines, and scaling strategies.

4. **Security and Compliance**: Understanding the data privacy and protection requirements (such as GDPR, HIPAA) and other compliance measures is very important when planning for migrations to make certain that data is dealt with securely during the entire process.

With regard to the data itself, data profiling analyzes content, relationships, distributions, and the basic structure at a more granular level. This helps to shed light on:

- **Data Distribution**: Data spread across tables, records, and categories helps identify data anomalies and areas that need transformation.

- **Data Redundancy**: The existence of duplicates or unneeded data storage inefficiencies. This aids in the decision to consolidate and simplify the data model.

- **Anomalies and Gaps**: Issues with data such as the absence of needed values, incorrect values, or inconsistencies from one data source to another, which need to be fixed prior to migration.

Informed decisions regarding legacy data and their optimal migration strategy can be developed when firms properly assess and profile their data.

Practical tools and techniques commonly used for assessment and profiling include:

- **Enterprise ETL/Data Integration**: Talend, Informatica PowerCenter, and Microsoft SSIS.

- **Data Quality and Validation**: Great Expectations, Deequ, and Monte Carlo (observability).

- **Transformation and Modeling**: dbt (for ELT-style transformations and tests) and SQL-based refactoring.

- **Cataloging and Lineage**: Collibra, Alation, Apache Atlas, and cloud-native lineage services.

Assessment outputs should directly inform the modernization strategy—for example, high defect density and schema rigidity typically justify refactoring, while stable, well-documented datasets may be suitable for lift-and-shift in early migration waves.

Table 13-1. *Sample data profiling snapshot (illustrative)*

Dataset/ Field	Observed Issue	Example Finding	Recommended Action
Customer. Email	Completeness gap	7.4% null values	Impute/collect missing; enforce NOT NULL where applicable
Orders. OrderDate	Anomaly/invalid values	Dates in the future (0.8%)	Apply range checks; quarantine invalid rows
Products. SKU	Duplicates	1.9% duplicate SKUs	Deduplicate; create unique constraint; reconcile sources
Payments. Amount	Outliers	Extreme values beyond 99.9th percentile	Winsorize or investigate fraud/ETL defects

Selecting the Right Data Modernization Strategy

As noted earlier, modernizing data presents a multiplicity of approaches, each with its own pros and cons. Choosing the most appropriate one is essential in modernizing successfully.

Lift-and-Shift Migration

The lift-and-shift approach is arguably the easiest approach to data migrations. Simply put, it means to relocate data to new infrastructure or the cloud from legacy systems with minimal changes. Such an approach is often considered for quick migrations or when there is a need to reduce risks of operating outdated systems.

Lift-and-shift migrations are less expensive and quicker than, for instance, refactoring migrations. However, they provide the least opportunity for improvement. In using this approach, you retain legacy systems for the most part and, hence, inherit the limitations and inefficiencies they pose.

Refactoring and Evolving the Schema

Refactoring and evolving the schema is an approach that is more advanced and involved as compared to "lift and shift." Moving and transforming data to meet a new system's needs is a part of this approach. Among the activities that this approach entails are

- **Scheme Modifications**: To better accommodate modern workloads and offerings, legacy systems schemes are optimized and modified.

- **Data Cleaning and Enrichment**: Covering legacy issues of data quality, data is updated to meet the new business requirements.

- **Modern Technology Integration**: For instance, from relational to NoSQL databases or adding cloud-to-serverless computing.

Though the benefits of this approach are more valuable in the long run, it can take a long time to complete and also often proves to be complex, necessitating ample planning and testing.

Real-time vs. Batch Data Migration

Real-time and batch data migration strategies serve diverse operating needs.

- **Real-time Data Migration**: Modern and legacy systems data sync in real time. Real-time migration is critical for deployments that operate 24 x 7, and for businesses that seek to cut down even the slightest of downtimes during migration.

- **Batch Data Migration**: As opposed to real time, batch migration moves large datasets after a fixed interval. While batch migration tends to have data sync lags or downtime, it is more fitting for systems with lenient migration schedules.

Real-time or batch migration selection depends on service-level requirements, data size, and business risk appetite.

Table 13-2. *Comparison of common migration/modernization approaches*

Approach	Typical Use Case	Advantages	Trade-offs/Risks
Lift-and-Shift	Fast relocation to the cloud with minimal change	Lowest disruption; quick timeline; preserves existing interfaces	Carries legacy constraints; limited performance/architecture improvement
Refactoring/ Schema Evolution	Modernize the data model and pipelines to fit the target platform	Improves quality, performance, and long-term agility	Higher effort; needs strong testing, governance, and stakeholder buy-in
Real-time (Continuous) Migration	24×7 systems requiring minimal downtime	Near-zero disruption; supports parallel run and gradual cutover	Higher complexity; requires CDC, conflict handling, and observability
Batch Migration	Large datasets with flexible cutover windows	Operationally simpler; cost-efficient for bulk transfers	Data lag; downtime/ cutover planning; potential reconciliation overhead

Data Transformation and ETL Pipelines

The transformation of data is initiated as soon as the migration process is completed. Data transformation is needed to modernize applications, as it is critical to their functioning. The evolved legacy data can be created with the ETL (extract, transform, and load) process that legacy data undergoes.

Let us explore the necessity of automated and scalable ETL pipelines in this section. Assimilation can be optimized by AI-driven automation from end to end by

- **Extracting Data**: Data extraction across varying formats and systems is automated, ensuring that disruption during extraction is kept to a minimum.

- **Transforming Data**: Data relationships, dependencies, and transformations required can be automatically identified, which can be driven by predefined business rules.

- **Loading Data**: The loading process is automated to eliminate errors and ensure that data is loaded to the target system or storage format.

Aligning faster and more efficient data transformation with business objectives is made possible through the use of AI and contemporary tools.

For large-scale environments, organizations typically choose between full (one-time) ETL and incremental ETL:

- **Full ETL:** It is appropriate for initial seeding or low-change datasets; requires larger cutover windows and heavier reconciliation.

- **Incremental ETL/CDC-Driven Loads**: It is preferred for high-velocity systems; it moves only deltas, reduces migration risk, and enables parallel run until cutover.

Modern ETL/ELT stacks often combine orchestration, transformation, and validation components—for example, Apache NiFi or Airflow for orchestration, dbt for SQL-based transformation and testing, and cloud-native services such as AWS Glue, Azure Data Factory, or Databricks for scalable execution and governance.

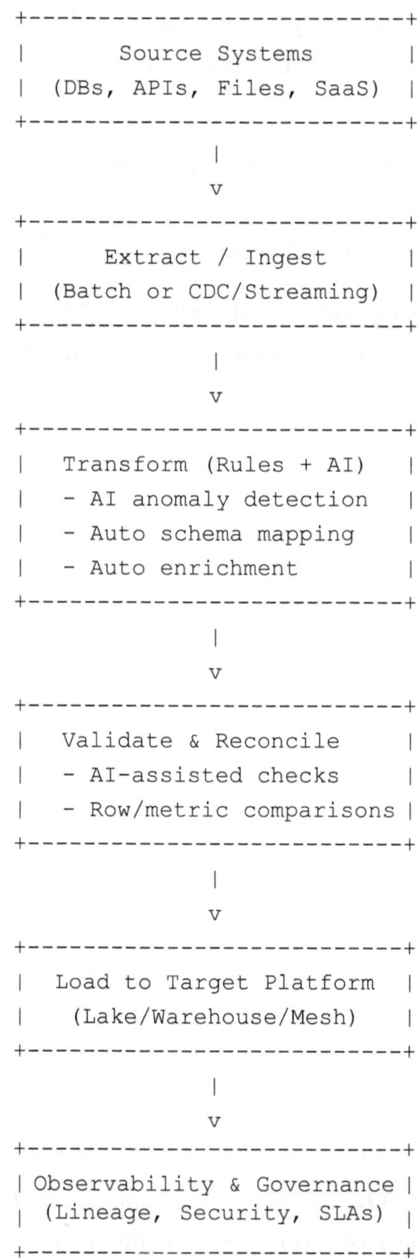

Figure 13-2. *AI-Enhanced ETL/ELT Pipeline Flowchart (conceptual)*

The Challenges of Modern Data Management

To address modern businesses' data needs, appropriate databases of the right type must be employed. The term "polyglot persistence" is used to describe the simultaneous employment of several different types of databases, such as relational databases and NoSQL databases, within the same system, as well as the needs being addressed by the system. Organizations can create an agile data architecture by addressing the stated needs with the appropriate system using different types of databases. Similarly, modernizing data management systems through the use of cloud-native technologies, as well as the use of microservices with containers and containerized databases, improves the capabilities offered.

Mini-case Example: Polyglot Persistence with Microservices (Illustrative)

A typical digital commerce platform may adopt polyglot persistence to optimize performance and scalability across domains:

- **Orders and Payments**: A relational database (e.g., PostgreSQL) for ACID transactions and strong referential integrity

- **Product Catalog and Personalization**: A document store (e.g., MongoDB) for flexible schemas and rapid iteration

- **Clickstream and Telemetry**: A streaming + time-series stack (e.g., Kafka with a time-series database) for high-ingest observability data

- **Search**: An index engine (e.g., OpenSearch/ Elasticsearch) to support low-latency queries and relevance ranking

While this improves fit-for-purpose storage, it increases integration complexity. Successful adoption therefore requires clear domain ownership, schema governance (data contracts, versioning, and a schema registry), and shared observability standards to prevent drift across services and datasets.

Cloud Data Service Integration

Cloud data services bring in different data management tools, automation, and scalability. This section illustrates the methods in which organizations can use cloud data services within their data modernization strategies. The primary services are

- **Data Lakes**: For storing large volumes of unstructured data for processing and deeper analysis

- **Data Warehouses**: For optimizing structured data for reporting and querying

- **Analytics and Machine Learning**: For deploying AI/ML models and getting insights in real time using cloud-based analytics services

With the integration of cloud services, firms can process data effectively and position themselves to make prompt decisions and innovate.

Best Practices and Lessons Learned

From the previous section, it is evident that the core themes and aspects are grounded in data migration and data integration, technology scaling, and effectively managing the rationalization of data stacks. The key ideas that strictly deal with the best practices include the following:

- **Stakeholder Communication**: Effective communication with and updates to C-level executives and business stakeholders, as well as IT and strategy teams, enable goal, timeline, and expectation management to be met.

- **Validation and Testing**: Carrying out and overseeing end-to-end validation and testing to guarantee that data is accurate and complete post migration.

- **Incremental Migration**: Migrate data in phases to reduce the risk and impact on data availability.

This section is critical, as it enables the readers of this guide to learn from the previous mistakes and ensure that they are avoided in future attempts at initiating data modernization efforts.

Cross-team Coordination and Operational Readiness (Practical Guidance)

Modernization efforts are rarely successful without explicit coordination across DevOps, data engineering, analytics, security, and business stakeholders. Practical coordination steps include:

- Define a single migration runbook with responsibilities (RACI) for cutover, rollback, and incident response.

- Establish shared definitions for data SLAs/SLOs (freshness, completeness, latency) and decision-making thresholds for cutover.

- Align infrastructure delivery (IaC), data pipelines, and downstream consumption teams on release cadence to avoid breaking changes.

Observability is equally critical. Instrument migration and ETL/ELT pipelines with metrics (row counts, error rates, latency), logs, and lineage so that defects are detected early and traced quickly to their source (e.g., transformation step, schema change, or upstream data drift).

Modernization Success Checklist (Use During Planning and Execution):

- Inventory and classify datasets (criticality, sensitivity, owners).

- Complete assessment/profiling and agree on acceptance criteria for data quality.

- Select migration pattern (lift/refactor/real time/batch) per domain and define migration waves.

- Implement automated testing (unit tests for transformations, reconciliation checks, and sampling).

- Establish governance (catalog, lineage, schema contracts, and access controls).

- Enable observability (dashboards/alerts) for pipelines and platform health.

- Perform phased cutover with rollback plan and stakeholder communication plan.

- Validate downstream reports/models and monitor post-cutover stabilization.

- Document lessons learned and update runbooks for the next migration wave.

Summary

To survive in today's world, any company must modernize their data. The suggested strategies for a company to adopt to modernize include schema evolution, AI-driven ETL, and cloud data services. Adopting these strategies enables a business to be more agile with data, scale operations much easier, and increase efficiency. The problems associated with outdated systems of data do not have to remain problems; instead, they can be solved with deliberate planning. In this chapter, useful strategies in constructing a contemporary, robust data infrastructure that aligns with the company's future plans and encourages innovations are provided.

CHAPTER 14

Event-Driven Modernized Applications

Introduction

As an application for the modernization approach, event-driven architecture (EDA) has gained notable attention in recent years. As the need for advanced digital services increases, traditional monolithic applications are often unable to meet the new requirements or scale appropriately. EDA addresses this issue by offering a more adaptable and scalable application development approach. Applications can respond to events as they occur, handle data asynchronously, and improve the performance of the entire system.

The objective of this chapter is to examine the principles and elements of event-driven applications, with a direct focus on event producers and consumers, alongside streaming platforms. In addition, we intend to explore the ways in which companies may construct event-driven microservices and make use of Event Sourcing and CQRS, advanced by the evaluation of asynchronous and real-time processing trade-offs.

© Mrinmoy Aich and Diganta Sengupta 2026
M. Aich and D. Sengupta, *Cloud-Native Modernization Unleashed,*
https://doi.org/10.1007/979-8-8688-2379-4_14

After reading this chapter, readers will know the basics of event-driven systems, appreciate their strengths, and be able to design applications built on the principles of the event-driven architecture.

Understanding Event-Driven Architecture (EDA)

Event-driven architecture (EDA) is a design methodology in which applications are developed for the receipt and further distribution of notifications. Events may include any notable change or happening in the system and may be customer registration, an order, or even the successful processing of a payment.

In a system dependent on events, the interactions of the different components are determined by the generation of notifications by some components to a messaging layer such as an event stream or a message queue. Other components or services may subscribe to such notifications to perform the designated operations in response. Such relations lack direct coupling between the consumers and the event producers.

The following are the key characteristics of EDA:

- **Loosely Coupled**: Allows event producers and consumers to be loosely coupled so that systems can scale seamlessly and independently.

- **Asynchronous Communication**: Events are mostly addressed asynchronously, leading to improved system performance and scalability.

- **Data Flow in Real Time**: EDA supports real-time event processing, allowing you to respond instantly to data or state changes.

This style of architecture provides several advantages, including improved scalability, responsiveness, and agility, which makes it perfect for cloud-native and modern microservices-based applications.

Event Producers and Consumers

In an event-driven system, there are two core entities: event producers and event consumers.

- **Event Producers**: Event producers consist of services or components that produce events. They can include user actions such as a customer placing an order or automated actions such as a cron job initiating a backup. They publish events to a messaging system such as Kafka or RabbitMQ, which in turn provides those events to consumers.

- **Event Consumers**: Event consumers are the components or services that listen to and act upon events. Upon an event occurrence, event consumers can initiate other processes, perform business logic, or update systems. For example, a payment service reacting to an "OrderPlaced" event and processing the payment acts as an event consumer.

Example of Event Flow:

1. **Producer**: The consumer completes the purchase process on the website.

2. **Event**: The "OrderPlaced" event fires.

3. **Consumer**: The payment service consumes the "OrderPlaced" event and processes payment.

In this example, the messaging system facilitates communication between the producers and consumers. As such, the producers and consumers are not aware of each other's existence.

Event Streaming Platforms (Kafka, RabbitMQ, etc.)

Event-driven applications use event streaming platforms to handle the events flowing from producers to consumers. Event streaming platforms offer the infrastructure needed for publishing, subscribing, and processing events in large volumes.

Popular Event Streaming Platforms:

- **Apache Kafka**: Kafka is an open-source event streaming platform used in event-driven systems. Kafka offers comprehensive publishing and subscribing services for streams of events, which are distributed, fault-tolerant, and scalable. Kafka is well known for high-throughput event streaming, which enables, as a result, both real time and batch processing.

- **RabbitMQ**: Another well-known messaging system is RabbitMQ, which supports asynchronous communication between services. Unlike Kafka, which focuses on event streaming, RabbitMQ offers messaging queue systems, where messages are put into queues and are processed in order. It fits better with use cases where message ordering and guaranteed delivery are important.

- **Amazon Kinesis**: Amazon Kinesis is a fully managed real-time data streaming service. Kinesis enables the collection, processing, and analysis of large data streams in real time, making it perfect for applications with real-time data streaming requirements.

Comparison Table: Kafka vs. RabbitMQ vs. Kinesis

Feature	Apache Kafka	RabbitMQ	Amazon Kinesis
Type	Distributed log-based streaming platform	Message broker (AMQP-based)	Fully managed streaming service
Primary Use Case	Real-time streaming, high-throughput event pipelines	Task queues, pub/sub messaging	Large-scale streaming analytics
Delivery Semantics	At least once, exactly once (with Kafka Streams/ transactions)	At most/least once; strong routing guarantees	At least once
Ordering Guarantees	Strong ordering within partitions	Best-effort ordering per queue	Ordering within a shard
Latency	Low (depending on configuration)	Very low	Low to moderate
Throughput	Very high	Moderate	Extremely high (auto-scaling)
Persistence Model	Durable commit log	Message-queue persistence	24 hours to 7 days retention
Scalability	Horizontal via partitions and brokers	Requires cluster tuning	Fully managed horizontal scaling
Operational Complexity	High (cluster management)	Medium	Very low (AWS-managed)
Consumer Model	Pull-based	Push-based	Pull-based

(*continued*)

Feature	Apache Kafka	RabbitMQ	Amazon Kinesis
Ideal For	Event streaming, microservice backbones	Work queues, RPC, event distribution	Cloud-native streaming & analytics
Cost	Infra + maintenance	Infra + maintenance	Pay per GB ingress/egress

Key Features of Event Streaming Platforms:

- **Scalability**: The platforms can scale horizontally to handle increasing data volumes.

- **Fault Tolerance**: The platforms also provide built-in fault tolerance to ensure data is not lost in case of failure.

- **Real-time Processing**: Event streaming platforms provide the ability to process events in real time or near real time, enabling low-latency applications.

Orchestration vs. Choreography:

Aspect	Orchestration	Choreography
Control Model	Centralized controller	Decentralized, autonomous services
Workflow Visibility	Clear & explicit	Emergent & implicit
Complexity	Centralized complexity	Distributed complexity
Scalability	Moderate	High
Failure Management	Easier to handle centrally	Requires distributed compensations
When to Use	Complex business workflows	High-volume event-driven interactions

The decision on which event streaming platform to use would depend on specific use case requirements such as throughput, message ordering, and durability.

Event Schema Standards in Event-Driven Microservices:

A consistent event schema is essential for reliable event-driven communication, backward compatibility, and cross-service interoperability. Modern microservice architectures rely on schema definitions that allow producers and consumers to evolve independently while maintaining compatibility.

1. **Avro**

    Apache Avro is a compact, fast, binary serialization format widely used in high-throughput event-streaming systems such as **Kafka**.

    Key Characteristics:

    - Binary format ➤ lower network overhead

    - Schema stored in a central registry (e.g., **Confluent Schema Registry**)

    - Strong support for **schema evolution**—backward, forward, and full compatibility

    - Ideal for high-performance pipelines and cloud-scale event streaming

    Why Use in Modernization Projects:

    Avro allows legacy systems being modernized to continue producing older schema formats while new microservices can deserialize them correctly through schema evolution.

2. **JSON Schema**

JSON Schema is commonly used with **RabbitMQ**, RESTful event publishers, and lightweight event systems.

Key Characteristics:

- Human-readable

- Easy adoption and integration with JavaScript, Python, Java, etc.

- Supports validation, constraints, and documentation

- Ideal for microservices using REST ➤ Event Bridge ➤ Stream platform patterns

Modernization Context:

As legacy ERP/CRM services transition to async communication, JSON Schema provides an easy validation layer to ensure events are structurally correct before entering the event bus.

3. **Protobuf (Optional but Common in Real-World Systems)**

Protocol Buffers (Google Protobuf) are widely used in gRPC and high-performance environments.

Key Characteristics:

- Very compact binary format

- Strongly typed

- Versioning-friendly

- Excellent for real-time microservices that combine gRPC + streaming

4.   **Why Schema Standards Matter**

Requirement	Avro	JSON Schema	Protobuf
High throughput	Excellent	Good	Excellent
Human readability	Low	High	Medium
Schema registry support	Strong	Emerging	Moderate
Schema evolution	Excellent	Limited	Good
Use Case Fit	Kafka, Kinesis	RabbitMQ, API events	gRPC events

Designing Event-Driven Microservices

A microservice is an independent modular service that works together with other microservices to build an application. The focus of designing an event-driven microservice is to decouple the services and allow inter-service communication through asynchronous events.

Key Principles for Designing Event-Driven Microservices:

1.   **Service Independence**: A microservice should work independently without any direct service-to-service dependencies and interact via events.

2.   **Event Contracts**: Clear contracts are necessary so that suitable interaction between producers and consumers is possible without any issues. The events must be standardized and well documented with schema and format for the events.

3.   **Event Choreography vs. Orchestration**: Event-driven microservices can take two approaches to coordinating workflows:

a. **Choreography**: Every service is aware of the events it needs to subscribe to and simply subscribes and reacts to the events. There is no central controller, and the services cooperate by exchanging events.

b. **Orchestration**: In complex workflows, an orchestrator service takes charge of the event flows, controlling how services interact and the order of interactions.

4. **Eventual Consistency**: Given a set of services in distributed systems, strong consistency becomes difficult to achieve. With event-driven microservices, it is common to operate on the principle of eventual consistency, wherein the services are sure that consistency is achieved as a result of events being processed.

Designing for Failure:

Failures should be anticipated and handled effectively. The event-driven microservices should be designed to tolerate errors in processing events. For example:

- **Retry Logic**: Retry logic should be put in place to handle temporary failures.

- **Dead Letter Queues (DLQs)**: Events can be sent to a dead letter queue if the event processing fails, either for manual intervention or for processing at a later time.

Event Sourcing and CQRS Patterns

Two of the fundamental patterns in event-driven systems are Event Sourcing and CQRS (Command Query Responsibility Segregation).

- **Event Sourcing**: This pattern is characterized by capturing every state change as an event. In this case, the current state of an entity is not stored; instead, the sequence of events that resulted in that state is stored. The current state can be derived by replaying the events.

- **CQRS**: The CQRS pattern segregates the operations for reading and writing into different models. The write model takes care of commands (updates), whereas the read model services queries (data retrieval). This pattern is typically paired with Event Sourcing, where the event store serves as the source of truth.

Event Sourcing and CQRS empower the system to:

- Track the changes that have been made and thus provide better auditability.

- Optimize the read and write models separately and thus enhance performance.

- Scalability and resilience, particularly for systems with very high concurrency demands.

Real-time vs. Asynchronous Processing

One of the fundamental questions in an event-driven system is whether events should be processed in real time or delayed asynchronously.

- **Real-time Processing**: Real-time systems work on events immediately after the events occur. They are used in systems that demand very low latencies, such as fraud detection, recommendation engines, and monitoring systems.

- **Asynchronous Processing**: Asynchronous systems process events with some delay and usually in batches. They are used in data pipelines and in systems that have some tolerance for the processing delay, such as data aggregation or reporting.

There is a tradeoff in all of these approaches with respect to complexity, performance, and applicability. Real-time systems require immediate results and are thus more complex to implement, whereas asynchronous systems have simpler implementations and may offer efficiencies for processing that is not time critical.

Observability in Event-Driven Systems

Maintaining and troubleshooting event-driven systems require observability, which is essential. In a distributed system, observability helps determine the flow of events, locate failures, and measure the overall health of the system.

Main Elements of Observability:

- **Event Logs**: Keep a log of all events as they are produced, processed, and consumed. This helps to analyze the system and track its behavior.

- **Distributed Tracing**: Monitor each event's path through the system. This helps identify processing delays, failures, or performance bottlenecks.

- **Metrics and Dashboards**: Track and visualize
  performance indicators such as event processing time,
  number of events waiting to process, and lag time
  of consumers. This verifies the system is working as
  intended.

Event-driven architectures can be equipped with Prometheus,
Grafana, and Elasticsearch to enable system monitoring and alerting in
real time.

Use Cases and Examples

Event-driven architectures are implemented in various industries, with the
following being the industries and use cases:

- **E-commerce**: In an e-commerce platform, an event
  such as "OrderPlaced" or "PaymentProcessed" initiates
  distinct workflows in individual services (e.g., payment
  processor, inventory, and shipping).

- **Financial Services**: Events such as
  "TransactionCompleted" or "FraudAlert" in the
  banking domain trigger subsequent actions like
  sending notifications, conducting fraud checks, or
  freezing accounts.

- **IoT**: IoT devices create events such as
  "TemperatureChanged" or "DeviceStatusUpdated"
  that initiate workflows for the rest of the system, like
  notifying a user or adjusting system parameters.

With these examples, it is evident how event-driven architecture
supports real-time processing and enhances responsiveness.

Best Practices and Lessons Learned

There is a set of best practices to follow for event-driven architecture:

- **Ensure "Idempotency" in Design**: Design event consumers such that they can process an event multiple times without breaking.

- **Manage Event Versioning**: Maintain backward compatibility of your events and change management as your system and events evolve.

- **Implement Backpressure Handling**: Use buffering, rate limiting, and other techniques to ensure graceful handling of load spikes.

- **Focus on Decoupling**: Services should remain loosely coupled and use events as a communication medium— facilitating scaling and maintenance.

Conclusion

Event-driven architecture is a scalable event paradigm. From the patterns covered in this chapter, organizations using this architecture can modernize their applications to respond to users and business needs even more. On the other hand, maintainable applications are the best to use for responsive, user-driven, and business solutions.

The next step for application architecture is event-driven systems that provide real-time processing, improved observability, and advanced communication between loosely linked services. When equipped with proper tools and planning, organizations can properly leverage event-driven systems and innovate with ease.

CHAPTER 15

Cloud Cost Optimization for Modernized Applications

Introduction

Illustrative cost snapshots (example figures; actual pricing varies by provider/region and discounts):

- **Always-on Microservices Baseline**: 3 medium worker nodes running 24/7 equals $3 \times 730 = 2,190$ node-hours billed per month, before adding managed databases, load balancers, and observability. In these patterns, fixed "always-on" capacity and the data layer tend to dominate the bill even at moderate utilization.

- **Event-Driven/Serverless Pattern**: 50,000,000 invocations/month at 200 ms average duration equals 10,000,000,000 ms of billed execution time, plus

© Mrinmoy Aich and Diganta Sengupta 2026

M. Aich and D. Sengupta, *Cloud-Native Modernization Unleashed,*

https://doi.org/10.1007/979-8-8688-2379-4_15

downstream services (API gateway, queues/streams, managed databases). Here, per-request compute and platform services become the main cost drivers, and traffic spikes can amplify logging and egress costs.

- **Data-Intensive/Streaming Workloads**: continuous ingestion (e.g., telemetry, clickstream, IoT) can shift costs toward managed data systems, high-throughput storage tiers, and network transfer—so optimization must consider data retention, compression, and lifecycle policies as much as compute.

Cloud computing has introduced new opportunities and operational models for developing and deploying software. A growing number of entrepreneurs and small businesses are specifically targeting the microservices, cloud-native applications, and serverless constituency that cloud computing scales to. Despite the benefits offered, the cloud infrastructure also presents issues with cost and optimization. Infrastructure-heavy modernized applications can be quite costly when left unchecked.

In this chapter, we explore strategies and best practices for cloud cost optimization in the context of modernized applications. We begin by understanding the primary cloud cost drivers, then dive into resource optimization techniques that reduce costs without sacrificing performance. We will also cover monitoring, budgeting, governance, and the tools available to help organizations gain better visibility and control over their cloud expenditures. Finally, we discuss real-world case studies, best practices, and how to sustain cost optimization efforts over time.

Understanding Cloud Cost Drivers

Cost driver	Illustrative share (%)	Typical drivers/notes
Compute (VMs/containers/serverless)	40	Always-on baseline capacity, autoscaling thresholds, and instance sizing
Managed data stores (DB/cache/queues)	25	Provisioned throughput, replicas, backups, and high availability configurations
Storage (object/block/file)	10	Retention, tier selection, snapshots, and access frequency
Observability (logs/metrics/traces)	12	High-cardinality telemetry, verbose logging, retention periods
Networking & load balancing	8	Load balancers, gateways, NAT, VPN/peering, service mesh overhead
Data transfer / egress	5	Cross-AZ/region traffic, CDN origin pulls, API consumers, inter-cloud transfer

Figure 15-1. *Illustrative Cost Contribution by Category in a Cloud-Native Microservices Application (1-Month Snapshot)*

Multi-cloud/hybrid-cloud note: cost visibility and allocation often become harder when workloads span providers or data centers. Common cost inflators include duplicate tooling (multiple monitoring stacks), cross-cloud data transfer/egress, inconsistent discount models/commitments, and fragmented tagging/chargeback schemas—so governance and standardization are critical in multi-environment estates.

You cannot optimize cloud costs without first understanding the components of the cost of the cloud. Cloud cost factors, unlike on-premises infrastructure, where costs are constant, are dynamic and dependent on the cost of infrastructure usage.

Key Cloud Cost Drivers:

1. **Compute Resources**: Cloud providers charge for the use of compute instances—virtual machines, containers, and serverless functions—based on the CPU, memory, and storage consumed. Cloud costs, for example, are significantly affected by the number of instances running, their size, and their uptime.

2. **Storage**: Storage of data is another, and often the greatest, cost driver, especially for data-intensive applications. Cloud providers generally charge a fee determined by the volume of data stored, the storage type (e.g., object storage, block storage), and the frequency of access.

3. **Data Transfer**: Additional charges are often incurred with data transfer in and out of cloud environments. Although inbound data is usually free of charge, outbound data can incur significant costs, especially for high-traffic applications.

4. **Networking and Load Balancing**: Networking components hosted in the cloud, such as virtual private networks (VPNs), load balancers, and gateways, also contribute to costs. These costs can be lowered by optimizing network designs and by minimizing unnecessary traffic.

5. **Licensing**: Licenses are required for many cloud applications or services, including software as a service (SaaS), infrastructure as a service (IaaS), and platform as a service (PaaS). These licensing fees may be usage-based or per seat.

6. **Scaling and Provisioning**: The cloud's ability to scale resources dynamically is a key advantage. However, over-provisioning or failing to de-provision resources incurs unwarranted costs.

Being aware of these cost drivers helps organizations in identifying what resources can be optimized, what waste can be eliminated, and how to control the total cloud costs.

Resource Optimization

Effective optimization of resources is crucial in lowering cloud expenditures without influencing the application performance negatively. The following techniques maintain the balance between cost savings and efficiency while providing aid.

Auto-scaling and Right-Sizing

Auto-scaling offers some of the most remarkable aid when it comes to optimizing cloud resources; it entails the adjustment, during set periods, of the number of active instances in relation to the set traffic or load offer. Performing auto-scaling safeguards the engagement of compute resources, ensuring that resources are neither over-provisioned nor under-utilized.

- **Benefits**: Auto-scaling ensures that the system can manage peak loads during the entire process, even during the low-traffic periods that follow. It improves cost efficiency by dynamically adjusting the number of containers or virtual machines in existence.

- **Best Practices**:

  Use horizontal scaling (scaling out) and vertical scaling (increasing the resources of an instance) in tandem.

  Use auto-scaling with container orchestration platforms such as Kubernetes for better control.

  Set appropriate scaling thresholds to limit unproductive scaling operations.

  Right-sizing automates the selection of the right instance type and size based on application performance needs. This process ensures that resources are not over-provisioned, which reduces unnecessary expenditure.

- **Benefits**: Intelligent instance selection ensures payment for only the required resources. While over-provisioning is financially wasteful, under-provisioning can lead to performance and system issues.

- **Best Practices**:

  Continuously monitor instance utilization with native cloud tools (e.g., AWS CloudWatch, Azure Monitor).

  For predictable workloads, lock in discounts by using reserved or spot instances.

  As your application evolves and resource requirements change, review your instance types on a regular basis.

Tracking Expenses and Setting a Budget Cloud Spending

```
[Tagging/labels + account/subscription structure] → [Budgets] → [Spend alerts
+  anomaly  detection]  →  [Chargeback/showback  reports]  →  [Remediation
(rightsizing,  scheduling,  policy  enforcement)]  →  [Monthly  review  and  re-
forecast]
```

• Define a mandatory tagging standard (e.g., app, environment, owner, cost-center) and enforce it via policy/guardrails at provisioning time.

• Create budgets per team/service (monthly and quarterly) and connect them to automated alerts at thresholds (e.g., 50%, 80%, 100%).

• Turn on anomaly detection to flag unusual spend spikes (new resource types, unexpected egress, runaway logging).

• Establish chargeback/showback reports so teams see costs in the same structure as engineering ownership.

• Automate common remediations: schedule non-production shutdown, enforce idle resource cleanup, and trigger rightsizing recommendations.

• Review weekly (tactical) and monthly (strategic) to update forecasts, commitments (reserved capacity/savings plans), and the optimization backlog.

Where native tooling is insufficient, many organizations adopt third-party cost management platforms such as CloudHealth, CloudCheckr, or Apptio Cloudability to consolidate multi-account/multi-cloud billing, improve   allocation,   and   operationalize   FinOps   workflows.

Figure 15-2. *Practical Workflow for Cost Visibility and Control (Alerts, Tagging, Budgets, and Remediation)*

```
[Tagging/labels + account/subscription structure] → [Budgets]
→ [Spend alerts + anomaly detection] → [Chargeback/showback
reports] → [Remediation (rightsizing, scheduling, policy
enforcement)] → [Monthly review and re-forecast]
```

   • Define a mandatory tagging standard (e.g., app, environment, owner, cost center) and enforce it via policy/guardrails at provisioning time.

- Create budgets per team/service (monthly and quarterly) and connect them to automated alerts at thresholds (e.g., 50%, 80%, 100%).

- Turn on anomaly detection to flag unusual spend spikes (new resource types, unexpected egress, runaway logging).

- Establish chargeback/showback reports so teams see costs in the same structure as engineering ownership.

- Automate common remediations: schedule non-production shutdown, enforce idle resource cleanup, and trigger rightsizing recommendations.

- Review weekly (tactical) and monthly (strategic) to update forecasts, commitments (reserved capacity/savings plans), and the optimization backlog.

Where native tooling is insufficient, many organizations adopt third-party cost management platforms such as CloudHealth, CloudCheckr, or Apptio Cloudability to consolidate multi-account/multi-cloud billing, improve allocation, and operationalize FinOps workflows.

Tracking comprehensive cloud expenditure is vital for its effective optimization. In this regard, cloud vendors may have a variety of tools that can be used to monitor and contain spending while enabling organizations to see how their resources are being used along with the associated costs.

Tools for Monitoring Cloud Expenditure:

- **AWS Cost Explorer**: AWS offers comprehensive details regarding the use and cost. Cost Explorer enables the monitoring of past use and makes it possible to predict future expenditures based on the current use.

- **Azure Cost Management + Billing**: The cost management features in Microsoft Azure enable users to monitor the use of resources, set budgets, and get notified when the costs go beyond the set levels.

- **Google Cloud Billing Reports**: Google Cloud also enables the use of detailed reports that provide the use and expenditure of the services.

Recommended Steps for Monitoring Expenses:

- Establish cost alerts in order to get alerts when spending gets near to or goes beyond the budgeted figures.

- Use of tags and labels enables resources to be categorized and the use of them to be tracked by project, department, or application.

- Periodically check billing statements to find any portion of use that requires rectification or to investigate any billing spikes.

Planning a Cloud Budget:

Formulating a cloud budget is critical to maintaining expenses within the limits of what the company has. Budgets can be customized according to service or team, and costs can be dispensed accordingly.

- **Budgeting Best Practices**:

  - Utilize budget forecasts and historical data as a base to set achievable goals.

  - Take into consideration usage or traffic spikes that are seasonal in nature (e.g., product or marketing campaign rollouts).

  - Modify budgets following a review to reflect changes in usage.

Case Studies: Lessons on Cost Cutting in Modernized Applications

Case Study 1: Cost Optimization in an E-commerce Platform Company

An ecommerce company modernized its legacy application and migrated to the cloud using microservices. They also adopted autoscaling and right sizing of compute and data storage, which together lowered cloud costs by 35%. Furthermore, the company adopted serverless architecture for order processing, which eliminated idle compute and further reduced costs.

Case Study 2: Cost Savings of a Financial Services Application

A financial services organization implemented an integrated containerized and cloud approach to their core banking system. With the use of reserved instances and the optimization of network traffic, the firm lowered cloud spending by 40% monthly. In addition, the company adopted the use of cloud cost monitoring tools to trace usage and enforce budget and cost control policies, which has been helpful in achieving budget compliance in scaling operations.

Best Practices for Sustainable Cost Management

Table 15-1. *Ongoing cloud cost optimization checklist (governance, auditing, and ROI tracking)*

Cadence	Control/activity	Owner	Evidence + ROI metric
Weekly	Spend anomaly review + top offenders triage	FinOps + Service owners	Anomaly tickets closed; % spend explained within 48–72 hours
Biweekly	Rightsizing and autoscaling tuning for top compute services	Platform/SRE	Cost per request/cost per transaction trend; utilization targets met
Monthly	Commitment planning (reserved capacity/savings plans) for predictable workloads	FinOps + Engineering leadership	Coverage rate; realized discount vs. on-demand baseline
Monthly	Tagging compliance audit and chargeback/showback reporting	Cloud governance	Tag coverage %; unallocated spend %; cost-center accuracy
Quarterly	Architecture review: data movement, caching, storage tiering, and egress minimization	Architecture board	Egress trend; storage tier mix; latency vs. cost trade-off documented
Quarterly	Security/compliance audit for cost-impacting controls (policy enforcement, logging retention)	Security + Compliance	Audit findings; policy violations reduced; cost of controls vs. risk rationale

Implementation Note: Track optimization ROI as a measurable delta (e.g., baseline monthly run rate minus post-change run rate), and keep an audit trail linking each savings action to a ticket/change request, owner, and verification window to prevent regressions.

For effective cloud cost optimization over time, cloud expenses must be effectively managed. This management includes the following:

1. **Continuous Monitoring**: The usage patterns of cloud services are bound to change over time; therefore, changes in cost-cloud inefficiencies must be monitored and optimized regularly.

2. **Performance and Cost Optimization of Resources**: Balance the costs against the performance needs by selecting the appropriate instances, storage types, and other resources.

3. **Utilizing Discounts from Cloud Providers**: Make use of reserved instances, spot instances, and other long-term commitment discounts from cloud providers.

4. **Automating Optimization of Costs**: Use appropriate automated scripts and policies to enforce cost-saving actions such as the shutdown of unused resources.

Final Words

Linkage to earlier chapters: data modernization and migration strategies can materially reshape cloud cost structures. For example, refactoring to managed services may reduce operational toil but introduce higher consumption-based charges; re-platforming can increase cross-service data movement; and migration-time data replication can temporarily inflate storage and egress. Accordingly, cost optimization should be treated as a parallel workstream throughout modernization—especially during data platform redesign, cutover planning, and post-migration stabilization.

Cost optimization lifecycle (repeat continuously): Identify ➤ Optimize ➤ Monitor ➤ Automate ➤ Review.

Modernizing applications and scaling cloud infrastructure come with a plethora of opportunities, of which cost optimization is a continuous and evolving process. To achieve the benefits of modernized cloud infrastructures at lower costs, organizations must closely monitor cost drivers and implement adequate measures to balance performance, scalability, and cost. With the deployment of such cost-effective resource optimization techniques as discussed in this chapter, the use of cost monitoring tools, and the availability of strong governance policies, organizations stand a better chance to reduce cloud expenditures while enjoying the flexibility and agility of the cloud environments.

Organizations can remain assured that their cloud infrastructure is cost-effective in the long run when cloud infrastructure best practices are followed, cloud usage is periodically reviewed, and cloud resources are effectively managed. With these controls, companies can more readily achieve their business goals at a lower cost.

CHAPTER 16

Testing Strategically for Modernized Applications

Introduction

Change management impacts testing as much as it does development. Testing adapts as we leave behind batch jobs for streaming and static virtual machines for ephemeral containers. New ways of delivering software—continuous delivery instead of manual releases—bring with them new ways for something to fail, new ways things can slow down, and new rules to follow. Old monolithic systems no longer work with microservices, and going from a single long-lived release train to many short-lived feature branches no longer works with traditional integration systems testing on a long-lived staging environment.

This chapter offers a complete and hands-on approach to testing modernized applications. It addresses unit, integration, and end-to-end (E2E) testing; contract testing for both synchronous and event-driven interfaces; automated quality gates in CI/CD; performance and security testing; test data management; and proven best practices. In all cases, we

© Mrinmoy Aich and Diganta Sengupta 2026
M. Aich and D. Sengupta, *Cloud-Native Modernization Unleashed,*
https://doi.org/10.1007/979-8-8688-2379-4_16

assume cloud-native infrastructure (containers, serverless, managed data services), polyglot persistence, and event-driven service interactions. We also assume the governance mechanisms discussed in earlier chapters: policy-as-code, evidence generation, SLO-based acceptance, and optionally agentic AI that suggests tests, curates data, and compiles audit documentation.

Our Main Objective: Rely on risk-based inference, observability, and automation-led testing tools to deliver rapid developer feedback, objective release decision triggers, and continual compliance documentation, all without hindering the pace of innovation.

Understanding Testing Challenges in Modernized Systems

Testing has changed. Entirely new challenges arise with the modernized, cloud-based infrastructure:

- **Ephemeral Environments and Serverless Compute**: Containers and serverless functions spin up and down frequently. Test setup to teardown has to be automated and idempotent, replacing "it worked on staging" with "it passes in an ephemeral, production-similar sandbox."

- **Distributed Boundaries and Eventual Consistency**: A single user transaction can touch multiple UIs, APIs, queues, streams, and data stores. Consistency is temporal and observable over events, not instantaneous over databases. Tests have to assert invariants over time and over channels (request/response, messaging, and scheduled jobs).

- **Interface Volatility**: APIs and event schemas evolve rapidly as teams are autonomous. Without contracts and compatibility policies, tests become brittle and regressions overwhelm.

- **Polyglot Stacks**: Different languages, frameworks, and data stores increase the diversity of tools and require more coordination.

- **Observability Gaps**: Tests that fail without traces, metrics, or logs are difficult to investigate. Tests must be and should be first-class producers of telemetry.

- **Flakiness**: Concurrency, time, network uncertainty, and clock drift create intermittent failures. Flaky tests reduce trust and delay releases.

- **Cost and Speed Trade-offs**: Broad integration and load tests are expensive. You cannot run "everything on every push." Intelligent test selection and layered pipelines are essential.

Flakiness, cost, observability, interface volatility, and concurrency are just symptoms. To address these, clear policies for compatibility and rollout, explicit contracts, reproducible and hermetic test environments, and telemetry-rich execution are needed. The rest of this chapter will explain how those principles are translated to action.

Unit Testing for Microservices

Priority of Test Execution: Risk-Based Approach

Another critical use of risk-based inference is that it enables the prioritization of the tests, particularly in an environment that is under the modernization process. Microservices are also complex and distributed;

hence, it is crucial to focus test activities on the most significant services whose effect on business operations is direct. Overall, user experience and revenue generation include microservices that are involved in the authentication process and payment processing. Such services should be more thoroughly tested, with the accent on the contract and integration of tests, in order to ensure their reliability and safety.

When deciding on the tests, it is possible to make sure that the exposure to the business risk depends on the cost of testing and flakiness. It runs the risk of tardy, flaky tests and wide-ranging integration tests that may find the company in the danger of service outage, security assaults, or tarnished customer satisfaction. To overcome this, groups should employ layered testing, i.e., less risky services should be tested with less rigorous tests and more rigorous tests in important business segments. This way, the resources can be more effectively allocated, and the quality assurance that is demanded is retained.

What to unit test. Unit tests validate pure behavior in isolation: domain logic, input validation, serialization/deserialization, error handling, and edge cases. They should not start servers, call the network, or require databases. Keep them fast (milliseconds), deterministic, and plentiful.

Patterns that help:

- **Hexagonal (Ports and Adapters)**: Put business rules behind interfaces; use in-memory fakes in unit tests and real adapters in higher layers.

- **Property-Based Testing**: Generate input distributions to discover edge cases (e.g., commutativity, idempotency, monotonicity).

- **Mutation Testing**: Assess test quality by injecting bugs; add assertions until mutations are "killed."

- **Golden Tests for Serialization**: Lock wire formats and error payload shapes with golden files; fail loudly on breaking changes.

Test doubles:

- Dummy/Stub for trivial dependencies; Fake for simple in-memory stores; Mock sparingly to verify interactions (e.g., "must call audit log once on failure"). Over-mocking couples tests to implementation details—prefer observable outputs over internal calls.

Coverage as a signal, not a target. Aim for meaningful branch/condition coverage of high-risk code paths; don't chase 100% mechanically. Pair coverage with risk maps (hot paths, money flows, auth decisions).

Anti-patterns: Hitting the network or filesystem; relying on system time/timezone; asserting on log text; a giant "God test" that proves everything and reveals nothing.

Cross-service Integration Testing

Integration testing is done to verify the interfaces between, for example, the service and its database, the service and the message bus, and the service and another service, balancing fidelity and speed.

Span testing can be done with the following:

- **Componentized Testing**: brings up a service with real adapters (i.e., HTTP client/server, DB, cache), but with isolated dependencies (local DB instance, ephemeral broker), as well as validating REST/GraphQL handlers, ORM mapping, transactions, and error handling.

- **Consumer-Driven Contract Testing (CDCT):**
  Providers meet expectations consumers define
  (request/response pairs) synchronously. For async
  "contracts," event schemas and sequencing invariants
  are included, moving integration feedback earlier and
  limiting the need for heavy end-to-end.

- **Schema Registries and Compatibility Rules**: For
  events (AsyncAPI/Avro/JSON), broken compatibility
  is not allowed in CI. Tests break when a new schema
  breaks registered consumers.

- **Testcontainers/Ephemeral Infra**: Start up and shut
  down DBs, queues, and caches per test or test suite.
  This avoids shared flaky staging dependencies.

- **Idempotency and Retries**: Integration tests need to
  verify retry/backoff logic and idempotent handlers,
  particularly in exactly-once-ish message processing.

What to assert:

- Protocol shape (status codes, headers, pagination, error
  payloads).

- Security boundaries (authn flows, scopes/claims,
  RBAC/ABAC enforcement).

- Transactional and consistency properties (at-least-
  once consumers are idempotent; outbox writes are
  aligned to domain events; read models converge).

When to call a real dependency. Real external services should only be
used if (a) a sandbox is available with deterministic data; (b) rate limits
and costs are acceptable; and (c) narrow stable behavior with assertions is
used. Otherwise, they should be virtualized.

Conducting End-to-End Tests and User Acceptance Tests (UAT)

E2E testing examines workflows that users directly interact with, chaining together the user interface, APIs, event triggers, databases, and notifications. Since they are resource-intensive, E2E tests should be minimal and well justified.

Choosing Scenarios: Pick the main and worst-case scenarios:

- Shopping cart checkout with a discount applied, including payment failure and retry.

- Account creation along with email verification and a password reset.

- Replayable, idempotent flows (e.g., double clicking on the "Pay" button and no double charge).

- Complying with regulations (data exports/deletions and consent changes).

Handling Instability:

- Prefer data attributes over CSS/XPath selectors.

- Use test-friendly clocks (time freezing) and eventual assertions (like "within 5s, UI shows shipment status").

- Seed deterministic fixtures; isolate tenants; clean up with "truncate + reseed."

- Capture trace IDs in the UI and propagate to services so failed E2E runs can be traced end-to-end.

UAT Cadence:

- Keep a consistent, tagged UAT build alongside release notes and test charters.

- Product, compliance, and support should be invited to run exploratory sessions with a focus on usability, accessibility (a11y), and policy acceptance.

- Control promotion with validation: passed charters, recorded sessions (if allowed), and defect burndown.

Visual Regression: For applications where UI is predominant, carry out baseline image comparisons on critical pages; permit low-noise thresholds and approve intentional deviations via snapshots.

Security and Compliance Testing

Testing Security and Compliance

The modern applications have security embedded in their makeup, and the aspect of security needs to be applied to the test process. We can integrate security and compliance as two distinct entities into the overall testing strategies instead of treating them as different entities:

Unit Testing: Small-scale security assertion has to be included in the unit test. These tests will have the capability of validating the input sanitization, the accuracy of the error management, and the proper parsing of authentication tokens to stem out the vulnerabilities like injection attacks in their early stages.

Integration Testing: In cases of interactive services, security and compliance checks should be even more notable. The flows or flow of authorization are to be checked in such a way that only the access-deserving users or services are granted to them. In the example of multi-tenant systems, integration testing should guarantee that data isolation is also guaranteed in addition to not allowing unauthorized access between the tenants.

End-to-End (E2E) Testing: E2E tests also ensure that evidence is gathered to be compliant in addition to being functionally correct. The tests are applicable in tracing and recording sensitive user activities such as logins, accessing, and transacting data, and this creates a record that cannot be modified later on audit. Particularly, it applies to the industries that are obliged to comply with the laws, including GDPR or HIPAA.

It is possible to ensure that security and compliance testing are not add-ons that are added at the end of the testing process by ensuring that they are part of each step of the testing process.

Resulting Benefits:

Cohesion: You include security and compliance in unit tests, integration tests, and end-to-end tests. By explicitly tying these two types of tests together, you form a story of how each of these types of testing is intended to deliver a secured, compliant system.

Clarity: The style does not present the readers with an impression of a segment of the puzzle, and they can clearly see how security is being incorporated in the whole testing process and not a solitary program.

Test Data Management and Mocking

The chapter is aimed at QA engineers, SREs, developers, and DevSecOps professionals who are interested in using the current approaches to testing cloud-native applications. It provides a generalized form of testing, which includes unit, integration, and end-to-end testing and covers the most significant core areas, such as security, performance, and compliance. It will equip practitioners with the practical techniques and practices to overcome the dilemmas of the distributed systems, temporary environments, and rapid pace of software delivery in the modernized infrastructures. Through this chapter, the readers will be in a position to get immense knowledge on how to guarantee high-quality, reliable, and secure software in the contemporary and complex world of the applications.

To make sure that modern applications can satisfy the functional and regulatory requirements, security and compliance testing is also needed. Nonetheless, managing to implement the concept of security throughout the testing lifecycle is challenging and has to be resolved with the help of data management policies and service reliance.

GDPR/CCPA Compliance: The testing should be done to guarantee that privacy laws such as GDPR and the CCPA do not discriminate in the handling of the personal data. This will involve hiding sensitive data in unit tests; the data retention policies must be upheld in integration tests, and full audit trails should be done in E2E tests. As an example, unit tests ought to be conducted with synthetic data that is regulated by the privacy rules, whereas E2E tests ought to make sure that all the personal data processing (e.g., consent management, data access) is in line with the compliance policies.

Dynamic Data and Ephemeral Services: The microservices are implemented in ephemeral environments, where it is essential to preserve the consistent and secure test data at all times. The problem of testing serverless services or services that are dynamically scaled could be addressed through synthetic test data and the use of mocking services in the previous levels of testing. It is also possible to use data snapshots or versioned test data as a steady basis for integration and E2E testing.

Service Virtualization vs. Real Dependencies: In testing interactions with third-party services or external systems, testing teams have to choose whether to use service virtualization or use real services. Although mocked services are good to use in unit and integration tests because they are fast and reliable, real dependencies must be used in high-risk areas of integration (e.g., payment processing or authentication) to make sure that contracts and integrations are tested with real service behaviors.

Flow of Test Data:

The nature of the data utilized changes as the testing becomes unit testing and E2E testing:

Unit Tests: Use artificial or masked data in order to be able to test logic correctly, but without using actual user data.

Integration Tests: Use a combination of masked data on most of the services and live data on important integrations in order to get interoperability between the services and not to jeopardize privacy.

E2E Tests: Full workflows in live data with adequate privacy standards (e.g., sensitive fields masked) are tested.

The testing process assures the compliance of applications with the stringent privacy/security expectations of modern regulations in conjunction with the functional requirements by aligning them to the principles of security, compliance, and data management.

Benefits:

Cohesion: The chapter shall now demonstrate how security and compliance testing is part of each stage of testing, from unit testing to E2E testing.

Practicality: The fact that mitigation options are introduced and a flow diagram is provided to users renders the testing process more practical, as it enables the readers to find their way through issues associated with compliance, data handling, and service dependencies.

Testing often runs into problems with data. Realistic, compliant, and reproducible.

TDM Strategies:

- **Synthetic Datasets**: Generate with domain rules (e.g., valid card PAN Luhn checks, address formats, SKU catalogs) and realistic skew (Zipfian hot products).

- **Masked Subsets**: Sample from production and irreversibly anonymize/tokenize sensitive fields; keep statistical properties.

Data Management and Fixtures:

- **Versioned Fixtures**: Treat your dataset as code; version it against your test suites; update consciously via migration scripts.

- **Time Travel**: Allow clocks to be injected; capture time-dependent behaviors (subscriptions, renewals, interest accrual).

Service Virtualization and Mocks:

- Virtualize external dependencies with defined SLAs, profile latencies, and introduce latency and errors (timeouts, 503s, malformed payloads) accordingly.

- **Contract-aware Mocks**: generated from OpenAPI/ AsyncAPI with schema validation; fast failure upon drift.

- For a message broker, provide fake topics with at-least-once semantics; test consumer idempotency and deduplication.

Determinism and Isolation:

- One test = one tenant or namespace.

- **Database**: ephemeral containers per suite, reset either through snapshots or migrations; avoid shared schemas.

- **Golden Event Streams**: curated sequences (e.g., order ➤ payment ➤ cancel) to replay situations for convergence.

Imagine and describe your scenarios, making it an evolving catalog: "happy path checkout," "retry payment," "stockout with backorder," GDPR delete," "idempotent refund," and "partial outage of recommendations."

Best Practices and Lessons Learned

1. Follow a pragmatic pyramid for tests. Many fast, deterministic unit tests; one focused layer of component/contract tests; and very few E2E highest-level journeys. Resist the "hourglass" anti-pattern (too many E2E; too few unit/contract tests).

2. Make tests observable. Emit structured logs, traces, and metrics with correlation IDs. A failed test with no trace is actually a bug in your test harness.

3. Shift left compatibility. Break the build if an API or event compatibility violation is detected in a PR; do not ever resort to discovering breaking changes in a shared environment.

4. Treat infrastructure as a test subject. IaC modules shall have testing of their own: unit (policy checks), integration (spinning resources), and compliance (tagging, encryption, and RBAC).

5. Quarantine is a tool, not a dumping ground. Triage flaky occurrences fast; set a maximum threshold for quarantine debt; assign an owner and SLA.

6. Gate by outcome, not intent. Passing checks should translate to the user-observable outcome: SLOs, CFR, and MTTR. Have tests that are constantly green but have unhappy users? Your tests are in misalignment.

7. Prefer contracts to mocks. Contracts decrease coupling and scale across teams. Mocks are local conveniences; contracts are the organization APIs.

8. Test data must be codified. Version, review, and reference datasets as you would code. Behind-your-back data changes are stealth regressions.

9. Budget for perf work. Perf tests aren't a one-and-done deal. Track latency histograms and cost-per-txn trends on each release.

10. Security is continuous. Integrate SAST/SCA/DAST into the pipeline; use policy-as-code to stop non-compliant artifacts at an early stage; rotate secrets like mad folks.

11. Test in production via feature flagging. Gradual rollout, canary, and targeted user cohorts decrease risk and provide a much more realistic testing environment.

12. Automate evidence. Every gate should produce artifacts (reports, SBOMs, traces) that can be attached to the commit or release for audit and forensic purposes.

13. Keep local dev productive. Give them make/scripts to spin a service with fakes, run the fast test suite, and tail logs. If they cannot do that in minutes, they will do much less testing.

14. Train for failure. Have game days with chaos scenarios; use incident postmortems to fill in missing test coverage.

15. Measure test effectiveness. Beyond coverage stats, measure the rate of escaped defects, the mean time to detect, test cycle time, flake rate, and correlations between gate pass and production stability.

Common anti-patterns:

- "Staging will catch it." (It won't, or it will be too late.)

- "We'll test the happy path and move on. (Users don't live on the path of light.)

- "100% coverage equals quality." (It doesn't; assertions do.)

- "Mocks everywhere." (Leads to a lot of false confidence.)

- "One shared QA database." (Data contention and flakiness forever.)

Conclusion

Testing for modern apps is not a bigger version of legacy tests but an entirely different discipline. Distributed boundaries, transient infrastructure, and independent teams all come with requirements for contracts, observability, and automation at every layer. A healthy strategy bakes in speed (for fast unit and component feedback), fidelity (targeted E2E and performance verification), and assurance (security/compliance evidence and policy-as-code gates).

Treat tests as first-class citizens in your architecture: design seams that allow for testing, produce the right signals, and enforce compatibility at build time. Use data responsibly—synthetic whenever possible, masked when necessary, and always versioned and reproducible. Let your pipelines absorb the load, performing layered checks, progressive delivery, outcome-based gates, and (when relevant) employing agents to suggest missing tests, maintain contracts, and collate audit artifacts.

Index

B

Billing service
    payment flow, 86
    setup express server, 85
Bitbucket, 137
Blue-green deployment, 155, 157
B-tree, 111

C

Cache eviction policies, 197
Cache purging strategies, 198, 199
Caching
    application-level, 199
    CDN (L3), 195, 198, 199, 204
    database query, 199, 203, 204
    definition, 192
    distributed (L2), 194
    HTTP, 200
    local/in-memory (L1), 193, 196,
        197, 200–202
    strategy flow, 205
    write-through and
        write-behind, 200
Change data capture (CDC), 235
Change management, 291
Chatbots, 69, 181
Cloud-based analytics, 11, 15
Cloud-based infrastructures, 4
Cloud-based Kubernetes,
    153, 154
Cloud budget, 285
Cloud computing, 4, 7, 17, 19,
    150, 278

Cloud cost drivers
    case studies, 286
    checklist, 287
    contribution by category, 279
    factors, 279, 281
    inflators, 279
    resource optimization, 281, 282
    snapshots, 277, 278
    tracking expenses and budget
        cloud spending, 283–285
Cloud data services, 258
Cloud expenditure, 284
Cloud migration, 3
Cloud-native architecture
    AI strategy, 69, 70
    APIs, 63, 64
    characteristics, 58, 59
    definition, 57
    deployment model, 66
    microservices, 60
    monolithic system, 60, 61
    security, 67–69
    technology stack, 62, 63
    vs. traditional, 59
Cloud resource management, 181
Cloud services, 22, 186
Code modernization, 3
Command query responsibility
    segregation (CQRS), 273
Compliance agent, 220
Componentized testing, 295
Consumer-driven contract testing
    (CDCT), 235, 296
Container-based systems, 7

L

M

U, V

W, X, Y, Z